AYURVEDA for Health & Beauty

Published by :
Lotus Press Publishers & Distributors

AYURVEDA for Health & Beauty

Parvesh Handa

Lotus Press
4735/22, Prakash Deep Building
Ansari Road, Darya Ganj,
New Delhi - 110002

Lotus Press : Publishers & Distributors
Unit No. 220, 2nd Floor, 4735/22, Prakash Deep Building,
Ansari Road, Darya Ganj, New Delhi- 110002
Ph.: 41325510, 98118-38000
• E-mail : lotuspress1984@gmail.com
www.lotuspress.co.in

Ayurveda for Health & Beauty

ISBN: 81-8382-006-9

Printed & Published by : **Lotus Press Publishers & Distributors,** New Delhi-02

PREFACE

In modern era stress, pollution, unhealthy diet, hectic life style etc., factors have adverse effects on body and spirit. Ayurveda is the ancient health care system aimed at energetically harmonizing body, mind and soul. It is believed that Ayurveda was passed down from God Brahma to his angels and finally to human. The value of Ayurveda have been recongnised for last 5000 years and is the oldest healing science.

The principal aspects of ayurvedic treatments are diet, medication and proper care to eliminate doshas, known as the Tridoshas. Vata, Pitta and Kapha. Vata consists of two elements of the universe, namely, air and ether (Akash). Pitta is a combination of fire and earth (Teja) and Kapha—the combination of ether and water. According to this theory the balance of these is unhealthy (Rog). Ayurveda tries to determine which of the three doshas is responsible for the ill health. The present book is based on herbs and substances generally available throughout the country. Under the eight heads, simple home remedies have been described which are free from any side-effect. The book is an humble efforts to explain Nature's science and its technology in a simple way from a layman's angle. I request all health and beauty loving people to give trial to different Ayurveda treatments after reading this book.

Detail of important herbs useful for natural cure, various ingredients for making herbal preapations yourself, Digestive system of human body, Ayurvedica treatments for Acne, Scars, Blemished Spotty Skin, Diseases of skin and Hair, Hydrotherapy, Therapeutic Herbal Baths, Curing Genito-urinary and Reproductive disorders and number of drugless therapies for Emotional disorders have been described in detail in this book.

I am thankful to Dr. Ved Prakash, Head of S.D. Naturopathy Hospital, Ambala Cantt, Dr. D.S. Jaspal, President Indian Medical Association Haryana and Dr. Suresh Sharma MD (Obs. & Gynac) for cooperation.

Ms. Parvesh Handa

Contents

1

The Magic of Herbs

Aloe Extract

A popular botanical recognized for centuries as having beneficial medicinal properties including antibiotic, anti-inflammatory and wound healing. Aloe vera is used in cosmetic preparations due to its moisturizing, soothing and calming properties. It is excellent for dry and sensitive skins as well as for the treatment of sunburns and other minor burns, insect bites and skins irritations. Aloe extract is obtained from the aloe vera leaves and is also referred to as aloe vera gel. Aloe vera juice is the diluted version of aloe vera gel.

Aloe vera is an emollient and film forming gum resin with hydrating, softening, healing, anti-microbial and anti-inflammatory properties having strong moisturizing ability. It penetrates the skin, supplying moisture directly to the tissue, moisture regulation and absorb UV light. It has relaxing effect on the skin, making it beneficial for sensitive, sunburned and sun-exposed skins. In addition, it is found to be an effective component in emulsions formulated for dry skin. Apparently, aloe vera also has a synergistic effect when used in conjuction with other antiinflammatory substances. It increases the blood supply to the area of application. Aloe vera is constituted of about 95 per cent water and the remaining constituents include minerals, polysaccharides, amino acids and carbohydrates.

Alder (Alnus glutinosa)

This herb plant grows near water, where it can be assured of moist soil. It is commonly found on riversides and marshy ground. Shiny oval leaves of alder enjoy the reputation of curing dropsical conditions caused by disorders of the renal system. The infusion may be used as a lotion for cooling sore, tired feet and prevent fatigue when walking.

Almond

Ground almond are extensively used in face masks. It is good for nourishing and cleansing. The Almond seeds contain 45 to 56 percent oil, which is known as "badam rogan." The oil is very rich and used in various preparations for skin care.

Angelica

A large aromatic plant has drowny, triangular leaves and white or more rarely pale-purple flowers. Angelica in both extract and essential oil form, is a herb for the digestion, bringing swift relief from flatulene, colic and heart-burn. An infusion made from the leaves and chopped stem is a tonic, detoxifying and purifying agent. Principal constituents of this herb are volatile oil (about 1%), valeric acid, angelic acid, sugar and a resin called anglecin. Angelica extract is made from the seeds and the roots. It provides an excellent gargle for the treatment of sore tonsils and throats. The plant is used to flavour many alcoholic drinks.

ANGELICA

Arnica Extract

A botanical credited with wide variety of properties such as antiseptic, astringent, anti-microbial, anti-inflammatory, anti-coagulant, circulatory, healing and stimulating. Arnica extract is also considered excellent for an acne condition, is effective in gels and creams designed to treat damaged, reddened or tired skin. The extract is obtained from the flowers. Repeated applications may produce severe inflammation on sensitive skins.

Avocado Oil

Oil is obtained from the ripe avocado fruit and expressed from the seeds. Rich and nourishing with high vitamin contents. The pulp is used in face masks and the oil in nourishing creams. Avocado oil can function as an emollient and as a carrier oil in cosmetic preparation. Its skin-benefiting properties include bactericidal and soothing, particularly to sensitive skin. Avocado oil may mobilise and increase the collagen of connective tissue and keeps the skin moist and smooth in addition to have the treatment for minor skin conditions. In cosmetic formulations, it helps to stabilize oil in water emulsions and effectively used in cleansing creams, moisturizers, lipsticks, makeup bases, bath oils, sunscreen and suntan preparations. Avocado oil enjoys the highest penetration rate among other oils such as corn, soyabean, olive and almond. It consist constituents such as oleic, linoleic and linolenic acid, palmitic and palmitoleic acid, lecithin, phytosterol, cartinoids and a high concentration of vitamins A, D and E.

Balm (Melissa officinalis)

A fragrant woodland plant with dark green wrinkled leaves and small creamy flowers. It helps in the treatment of eczema , dry skin, and used in acne treatment formulations and products for blemished or sensitive skins. The herb is credited with calming, soothing, healing, anti-spasmodic, tightening, antibactericidal and circulation-stimulating properties. Its effectiveness is due to the constituents such as citral, citronella, linalol, geraliol and aldehydes. Balm mint oil has sedtive, anti-pasmodic and antiseptic effect. Its use sometimes may cause skin irritation.

BALM

Balsam Peru (Myroxylon pereirae)

It is a botannical attributed to strong medicinal actions, recommended for curing scabies and skin diseases. The herb is considered anti-bacterial and sulphur based; recommended for use on acne skin and eczema.

Basil (Tulsi)

An a romantic herb with white flowers and oval-shaped, shiny leaves. Medicinally, basil is a potent tonic whose effect is both stimulant and nervine. It is particularly good at arresting morning and travel sickness besides, an effective skin tonic, application in acne preparations and rich in vitamin C. Basil oil is often used as a carrier oil

BASIL

and its properties include stimulating, tonic, purifying and anti-microbial.

Babchi

A well known medicinal herb, used as laxative and anthelmintic (antiparasite). Seeds of babchi cure leucoderma (white patches on the skin).

Babool (Kikar)

Used to clean the tooth. The leaves help relieve prolapse of rectum. Useful in cough, asthma and pittuisis. Decoction can help prevent threatened abortion.

Blackberry (Jamun)

Berries are not only delicious but good for anaemia conditions as well. The leaves are mildly aperient and accredited with sound tonic virtues. An infusion is made and applied externally as a lotion to cure psoriasis and scaly conditions of the skin.

Blackberry extract is regarded as excellent for its astringent and tonic properties due to the high tannin content of the root, bark and the leaves. The leaf extract accredited with sound tonic virtues can be beneficially used for acne conditions. A standard infusion is made, which can be applied externally as a lotion to cure psoriasis and scaly conditions of the skin.

Betony (Chhitran Parni)

A purple-flowered plant, is a natural pain killer, especially good for headaches and neuralgia. It purifies the blood and cures acne and other skin disorders.

Birch (Betula-Bhoj Patra)

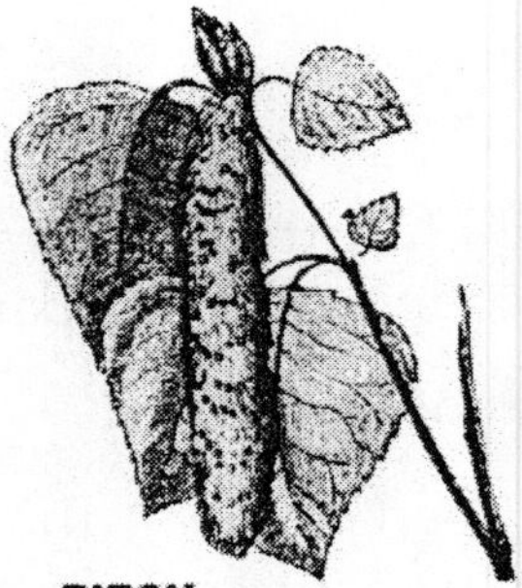

BIRCH

Birch extract has been described as astringent, antiseptic, softening, curative and circulation-stimulating. They are believed to have curative properties in case of skin diseases. Birch has healing effect on rashes and hair loss. The important constituents include glanonoids, hyproside, tannin, saponins and quercetin. Birch extract has anti-irritant and antiseptic properties and used in acne, eczema and sunburn treatment. The leaves of the plant have a peculiar, aromatic odour and a bitter taste which secrete a resinous substance with acid properties and contain flavonoids, tannins and essential oils.

Black Pepper Oil

It has cosmetic application, used on skin inflammations and superficial wounds. This oil is obtained from small-grains. The plant, usually is found in hilly areas.

Borage (Pattharchuri)

BORAGE

The plant with blue flower have both leaves and stem covered with white bristles. Borage has beneficial effect on heart, kidneys, adrenal glands and the entire digestive system. The herb cures jaundice and increases the milk flow in nursing mothers. Borage juice obtained from the crushed plant and applied direct to the skin cures ringworm. The tropical application of borage extract is described as antiinflammatory and beneficial for sensitive skin and allergic reactions. Borage contains potassium and calcium, combined with mineral acid. The oil extracted from seed is an effective anti-irritant and has hydrating properties.

Bergamot (Zabeer)

An aromatic herb, used to perfume colognes and toilet waters. Bergamot oil is considered an antiseptic and bacterial growth inhabitor, good for oily and acne skin and for seborrhoeic conditions. Sun exposure after applying pure bergamot oil may cause hyper-pigmentation and skin rashes on the neck area behind the ears.

BERGAMOT

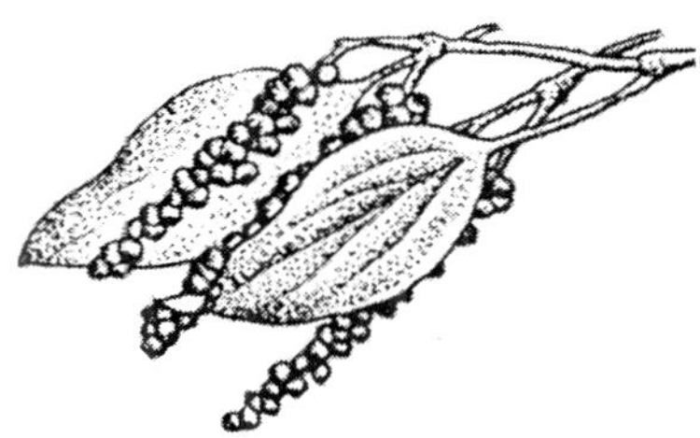

Carrot Oil

Derived from the carrot root, carrot oil is used since the 16th century for skin diseases due to its cleansing, depurative and draining properties. This carotene-rich emollient has been indicated for acne and skin conditions such as dermatitis, skin irritation, rashes and wrinkles. The root of this plant has nearly 89 percent water. The extract obtained from the carrot leaves have cleansing properties and healing effect due to its strong antiseptic qualities. The juice contains sugar, a little starch, albumen, volatile oil, vegetable jelly or pectin, saline matter, malic acid and carotin.

Calendula Marigold

Its flowers and leaves are very beneficial for clearing the skin of eczema, spots and grease. It is claimed to be rejuvenating. Calendula extract is an emollient said to have healing, soothing, antiseptic, anti-itching and antiinflammatory properties. Effectively used in case of oily and delicate skins as well as for curing acne. The extract is obtained from calendula blossom.

Comfrey

A plant with pinkish blue bell-shaped, contains allantoin and is credited with healing, astringent, and emollient properties. It is used in case of swelling, bruising, cuts, papules and pustules. The extract is traditionally used topically for soothing and anti-itching treatment (a cold compress for eye injuries), as well as for eczema and wounds. The herb contains from 0.6 to 0.8 percent of allantoin and a bit of tannin.

Celandine

The herb plant is found in hedgerows and wastes. Yellowish hairy leaves shaped like oak leaves and small yellowish flowers. As a wart cure the raw yellow juice should be applied direct to the skin. Some herbalists prescribe an eye lotion made from one part of this infused herb and two parts of water or milk.

Cleavers (lipatni ghas)

The plant has tiny white flowers and small round fruits. Cleavers are excellent remedy for diseases of the urinary system. An infusion of this herb, used as a lotion, makes a first-rate tonic for the scalp and the skin. It clears dandruff, cures leprosy and skin cancer. The extract is very useful in treating eczema and spots, and is recommended for normal to dry skins.

Clove (laung)

An aromatic spice used in skin tonics and stimulating face masks. It is considered as a powerful antiseptic with a strong germicidal effect. Clove oil may cause strong skin irritation when used in high concentration. The clove oil is obtained from the stems and leaves of the plant.

Camomile (Babuna -ka- paudha)

Plant with strong botanical properties and feathery grey green leaves, usually found in waster places. The plant has a distinctive smell similar to over-ripe apples. An infusion of leaves and flowers of this plant (fresh or dried) has wide cosmetic and medicinal uses.

Camomile dissolves tumors, heals ulcers, expels worms, banishes tiredness and treats many female disorders. As a cosmetic the herb can be used as a face-wash to clear complexion and as a rinse to lighten hair. Camomile tea is a tonic, digestive and tranquillizing. It is usually sweetened with honey. Camomile oil is credited with anti-allergic, healing, cooling, analgesic and antiseptic properties. It has been found exceptionally good for treating burns, skin inflammations and dermatitis.

Cinnamon Oil

Said to have a soothing effect on the skin. It is widely recognised for its tonic and antiseptic properties. It is obtained from the plant's leaves.

Cedarwood Oil

Credited with antiseptic, sedative and astringent properties. This clear oil is valuable for use on various skin eruptions such as relieves itching, cures acne and oily skin, helpful in case of dermatitis, eczema and psoriasis.

Dandelion (Kukraundha)

DANDELION

The medicinal value of the Dandelion plant with golden-yellow flowers is used to treat all kidney complaints, liver troubles and circulatory disorders. It is widely used for the treatment of arthritis, to disperse acidic deposits from the affected joints. It cures pimples and skin spots.

The dandelion extract has tonic properties, refreshes the skin, corrects pH balance, aids in increasing the respiratory capacity of the skin tissues, beneficial for dry skin and also used in acne preparations. The plant root is used for cosmetic preparations rather than the flower, as juice of the root is more powerful part of the plant. The main constituents of dandelion root are taraxaine (a crystalline bitter substance), taraxacsn (an acid resin), insulin, gluten gum, potash, crtric acid, sterols and vitamin B and C.

Elder (Elder Vriksh)

All parts of this herbal plant are used. Its leaves combined with honey is a standard infusion that clears troubled skin. The infused flowers offer a remedy for catarrh, cough and colds. It soothes burns and scalds. A balm of elder flowers keeps crow's feet at bay. The herb is said to have astringent, antiseptic and emollient properties. It is very useful for problem or inflamed skin and the ointment made from the leaves cure bruises, swelling and wounds. They are also

ELDER

ingredient in many cooling ointments. Elder flower extract is used for eye and skin lotions, particularly beneficial for treating dry skin. Elder flower water is used to clear the complexion of freckles and sunburn, and keeps the skin in good condition. Elder flower extract is used for eye and skin lotions, particularly beneficial for dry skin. Elder flower water is commonly used to clear the complexion of freckles, sunburn, and keeps the skin in good condition.

Echin Acea

Both oil and resin derived from the wood or the bark of this aromatic plant have antiseptic and anti-bacterial properties, helpful in treating skin lesions. It also has anti-itching and soothing properties when used in skin care products and is commonly used in anti-acne preparations.

Elm bark and Extract

Credited with astringent, healing and soothing properties that could benefit surface skin problems. Extract from elm leaves is usually recommended to wash wounds, bruises and sore eyes.

Eucalyptus

An antiseptic used to fragrance cosmetic preparations. Eucalyptus oil has antiseptic, disinfectant and blood circulation activating properties and is considered one of the most powerful and versatile herbal remedies.

FENNEL

Fennel (Saunf)

It is a herb which has a cleansing effect on the skin,

especially as a cleanser and detoxifier for oily skin types. When steaming the face, use it in the water. The principal constituents of fennel oil are anethol, fenchone, plus d-pinene, phellandrine, anisic acid and anisic aldehyde.

Fenugreek Extract

An emollient,anti-inflammatory and healing ingredient used in the treatment of irritated skin. The seeds of this annual herb have been used through the ages for medicinal and culinary purposes.

Garlic (lahsan)

Garlic is included in the same group of plants as the onion. Recognized as an antiseptic and bactericide. The garlic ointment externally applied, reduces hard swelling and for treating skin problem including acne. The active properties of garlic depend on a pungent, volatile, essential oil obtained by distillation. Rich in sulphur, garlic oil helps in clearing skin problems such as eczema and acne.

Geranium Oil

Has botanical properties described as refreshing, anti-irritant, mildly tonic and astringent. It is good for all skin types, particularly benefit oily and acne skins. This oil is used in perfumery and cosmetics.

GERANIUM

Henna (Mehandi)

An astringent herb with cooling properties. It is used for hair conditioning. Henna is a colorant that provides a reddish brown shade. It has important constituents which include mucins, phytosterols and napth-oquinones. The extract is obtained from the leaves.

Haldi (Turmeric)

It helps glow in skin when mixed to a face pack. It prevents inflammation, cures injuries, wounds, used for gonorrhea (Venereal Disease) and clears eyes relieving pain and redness.

Horse Raddish Extract

Traditionally used against sunburns, superficial and other non-extensive burns, and to give the skin clarity and freshness. Its antiseptic and skin clearing properties are linked to its ascorbic acid content. The extract is made primarily from the plant's roots.

Horsetail Extract (equisetum-ka-paudha)

General botanical properties include stimulating, astringent, soothing, healing and softening. Horsetail increases the skin's defense mechanism, regulates the skin due to the plant's rich mineral contents and strengthen connective tissue due to the presence of silicic acid. It works to prevent and counteract wrinkles in the eye area. It is beneficial in both anti-aging and relieving acnes.

Houseleek

An herb having healing and astringent properties. Ideal to cure warts and ringworm.

Hyssop Oil (Zufah Yabis)

Properties include healing, tonic and stimulating. It is indicated for dermatitis, eczema and wounds. This aromatic plant has long leaves and clusters of light blue flowers. It also regulates blood pressure, clears the chest, calms the nerves, improves digestion and protects the body form infection.

Ivy Extract

Ivy extract has a slimming and anti-cellulite effect due to its ability to prevent water accumulation in the skin tissue. It is considered antibactericidal and soothing, particularly in burn cases. Apparently, ivy also has detergent, anti-parasitic, decongestant and analgesic properties. The leaves are traditionally used to treat various skin eruptions, irritation, dermatitis and skin ulcers.

Jasmine Oil

A highly aromatic oil made from the flowers and used as a perfume. Jasmine may cause allergic reaction (swelling). The oil is credited with moisturizing, soothing and healing properties. It is indicated for dry and sensitive skins, and also for skin with dermatitis.

Lemon

Rich in vitamin C, it is used in skin tonics and creams. The botanical properties include as acidic, anti-bactericidal · and antiseptic. Lemon extract is suggested for treating sunburn, acne problems and

oily skin. This extract contains citric acid, vitamin B and C. Lemon oil is one of the most versatile essential oil, is considered a counter irritant, antiseptic, depurative and lymphatic stimulant. It is widely used in the perfume and soap industry. Lemongrass oil is the volatile oil distilled from the leaves.

Kaner (leander)

Plant with white, yellow and red flowers. Bark of the root cures many skin disorders and purifies the blood. Oil prepared from this plant is useful in case of scabies and ringworm.

Kalonji

Black seeds resembling onion seeds destroy intestine parasitis, benefits in cases of gall bladder, calculi, gout, rheumatism and sciatica. Ground in vinegar it helps leucoderma, ringworm, alopecia (patchy baldness) and acne on the face.

Juniper Oil (Hapusha)

Juniper oil is antiseptic, astringent, cleansing and toning. Also credited with good penetrating capabilities, and is considered helpful in treating acne (oily skin), dermatitis and eczema.

JUNIPER BERRY

Lavender

It has a pleasant fragrance and used for scenting bath water. Used as nerve tonic, curing cough, anti-paralytic and mouth wash. On external application soothes headaches, reduces inflammation. Properties include antiallergic, anti-inflammatory, antiseptic, anti-bacterial, anti-spasmodic, balancing, energizing, soothing, healing, tonic and stimulating. Lavender oil works on all types of skins and produces excellent results when used for oily skin as well as in the treatment of acne, burns, dermatitis, eczema and psoriasis.

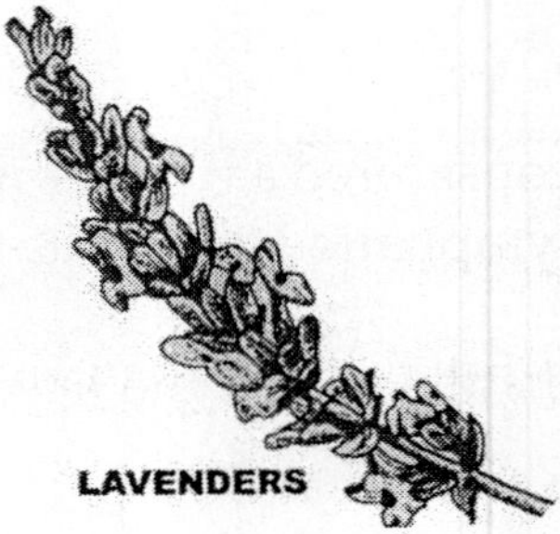

LAVENDERS

Lettuce (Chukandar)

Rich in minerals, iron and vitamins. It is cooling and excellent for sunburn to redness.

Marigold

The orange marigold is a prolific garden plant. It opens its petals at nine and closes them at four. A disinfectant herb, marigold is used in effective treatment of ulcers and open sores. The flowers may be eaten raw, taken as a standard infusion when applied as a lotion., The plant cures varicose veins and other circulatory troubles. As a lotion, a marigold infusion (petals only) provide the ideal balance of an over-oily skin and all complexions. It has antiseptic, healing and soothing effect and heals sunburns and skin rashes.

MARIGOLD

Marjoram (Marwa, Sathra)

Described as tonic and antifungal. Most popular for botanical applications, Marjoram oil is beneficial for antispasmodic, calming and sedative indicating applications for sensitive and irritated skin. Sometimes, it may cause allergic reactions with symptoms being skin redness and itching.

MAJORAM

Meadowfoam Oil

A rich emollient. It is widely used in cosmetic formulations because of its dryness and quick penetration into the skin. The extract has strong anti free radical properties as well as analgesic and topical anti-inflammatory activity. The plant grows abundantly at the edges of the river and ditches.

Mimosa

Used in cosmetics for its believed epidermic tissue regenerating, antiseptic, astringent, anti-inflammatory, repairing and protecting properties. Used effectively in postsun preparations, baby skin care creams and protective creams. It may sometimes produce allergic skin reaction.

Mint (Pudhina)

Has cooling, tonic, stimulating, antiseptic and relaxing properties. Mint was traditionally used as an adjunct soothing and anti-itching treatment. This aromatic herb is widely used as a fragrance in beauty products and serves as a cleanser for acne and dermatitis treatment.

Myrrh

Said to have disinfectant, antiseptic, antiinflammatory, anti-itching, cicatrizant, tonic, stimulant, sedative and astringent properties. Myrrh extract can be valuable in products designed for acne treatment. Myrrh an traditionally ancient ingredient for perfumes and incense, was used by ancient Egyptian women in facial masks and other cosmetic preparations.

Myrtle

An astringent and antiseptic with strong botanical properties suitable for acne and oily skin.

Neroli Oil

A fragrance, used in skin care preparations to stimulate cell regeneration. It leaves a sedative and soothing effect and must beneficial for sensitive, delicate and all skin types. True neroli is extracted from bitter orange blossom and is one of the most expensive oils, therefore is widely adulterated with the distillation of other citrus blossoms such as sweet orange, lemon and mandarin.

Nettle (bichchhubooti)

The botanical properties include as antiinflammatory, astringent, bactericidal, healing, mildly deodorant antio-xidant and stimulating. It is effective for treating eczema and sunburn. Nettle is the botanical with the highest vitamin E content. Nettle's important constituents include acetylcholine, amino acids, histamine, carotenoids and chlorophyll.

NETTLE

Oak

The botanical properties are described as slightly tonic, strongly astringent, antiseptic, soothing and anti-inflammatory. It reduces inflammation and prevents infection. Oak root is recommended for sensitive skin, protecting it against unwanted reactions such as swelling or redness.

Oat

Oat extract obtained from the seeds of oats has soothing properties on the skin. All oat grades enhance emulsion stability, increase viscosity, leave a smooth after feel and provide a source of whole natural vegetable protein. Oatmeal preparations are beneficial for irritated skins resulting from sunburn, psoriasis, or allergic dermatitis. The oatmeal relieves redness and itching. It acts as a soap-free cleanser and provide a gentle base for face masks designed to work with delicate, sensitive skin. This mask absorbs oil from the skin's surface and reduce the redness of irritated, broken-out skin. Oat flour is an abrasive, absorbent, bulking, and viscosity-increasing substance. It is used in a variety of cosmetic preparations including powders, masks, packs, moisturizers, suntan gels, hand and body creams and soaps.

Olive Oil

A carrier oil with excellent luricity, pale colour and low odour . Olive leaf extract is astringent and antiseptic, and also provides antioxidant and vasodilatant properties . It is used in anti-aging products .

Orange Flower Oil

Credited with soothing and calming properties when used in skin care preparations . The oil should not be confused with orange flower extract. The flowers from the bitter orange tree yield an essential oil known as neroli.

ORANGE FLOWER OIL

Palmarosa Oil

The properties attributed to this oil are soothing, moisturizing, antiseptic and cell regeneration. Its used for acne skin and dermatitis condition as well as for dry skin. The oil leaves immediate calming and refreshing action on the skin and is widely used in perfumery and cosmetology.

PALMORASA

Pimpernel

This little plant with small oval-shaped leaves, long slender stalks, bearing bright scarlet flower was popular since the ancient Greeks to treat eye diseases, jaundice, dropsy and inflammation. The plant has cosmetic value and is applied as a skin lotion to cure skin pigmentation, removing freckles and blemishes and acts as a hair restorer.

Patchouli Oil

Botanical properties of this herb are described as astringent, tonic, sedative, anti-inflammatory and decongestive. Its botanical

PATCHOULI

attributes make it useful for acne, aged and chapped skin, and skin redness. The oil has strong, sweet, musty and very persistent fragrance.

Peppermint

Credited with refreshing, cooling, bactericidal and anti-irritant properties. It is used as a fragrance, can produce allergic reactions such as skin rashes and irritation, helps relieve skin irritation and itching in extract form and reduces skin redness due to inflammation or acne.

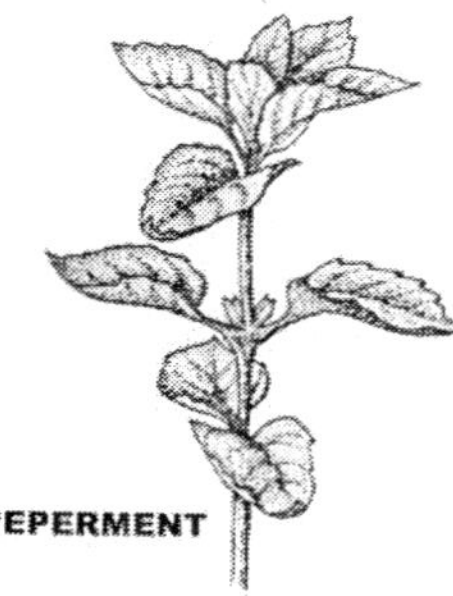

PEPERMENT

Petit Grain Oil (Petitgrain)

Widely used in pharmacy and perfumery for its therapeutic and tonic effect. It has fresh fragrance and credited with tonic and antiseptic properties.

PETITGRAIN

Pumpkin

Credited with purative properties. Cosmetic applications include use in acne products and as anti-seborrheic.

Quince

Obtained from the dried seeds, its extract is used in cosmetics for dry skin and eye treatment preparations. The seeds are an emollient, emulsifier and thickening agent.

Raspberry

Botanical properties are described as astringent and tonic. The concentrate is added to cosmetics to give them the fruit's fresh smell.

Rose

Rose extract rich in vitamin C is credited with astringent, tonic and deodorant properties. It is also used as a fragrance. Rose oil has moisturizing and moisture-retention, slightly tonic and soothing properties. It is helpful in case of skin redness or inflammation, when moisturization and regeneration is needed. Rose oil is beneficial to all skin types, particularly mature, dry or sensitive skins. This oil being most expensive essential oils, is largely adulterated with substances like geranium, lemongrass, palmarosa, and terpene alcohols. About 30 roses are required to make one drop of oil. Rose petal extract has mild astrigency and tonic value. Rosewater is credited with cooling, soothing , astringent, and cleansing properties. Rosewater is often mixed with glycerin which provides moisturization and lubricity. Rosewater oil is one of the major perfumery oils useful as a cellular stimulant and tissue regenerator, especially good to sensitive and aged skin, wrinkles, and general skin care.

Rosemary (Rusemary)

A popular garden plant with spiky dark green leaves and distinctive scent. As a medicine, it is valuable tonic for heart and liver and helps reducing high blood pressure. Rosemary is widely used in the treatment of

digestive disorders and menstrual pain among women. Used as a lotion, this herb relieves pain in the head and cough, when a spoonful of the herb mixed with honey and melted butter is taken. Rosemary is a fine tonic for the scalp and skin, adds lustre to the hair and is a useful ingredient in commercial shampoos. It helps to keep the skin free from the wrinkles. Washing the face with rose water keeps the youth alive. The extract has astrtingent, toning, stimulating, deodorant, antiseptic, reactivating, softening and invigorating properties which helps curing acne, dermatitis, eczema, thereby aiding in skin regeneration. The constituents of rosemary extract include amino acid, rosemary acid and apigenin.

Sage (Salvia, Sefakuss)

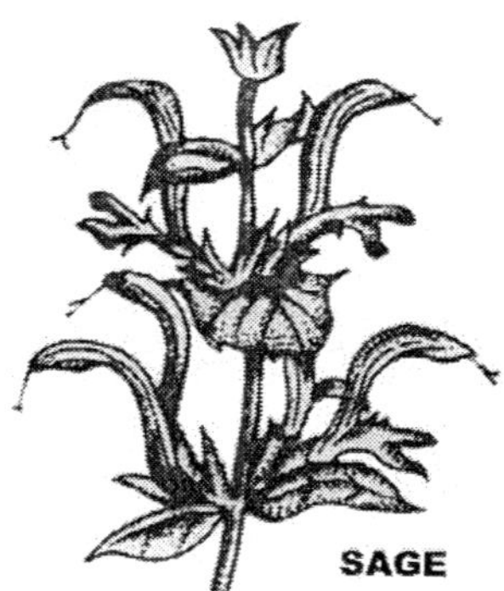

An aromatic, sun-loving plant with grey green leaves and mauvish flowers. The herb is used to treat cough, cold, headache, fever, troubles of the liver, bile and the digestive system. When used as gargle or mouth wash the herb helps to cure sore throats and gums. The lotion heals ulcers, sores and other skin eruptions such as acne and oily skin. Sage oil is credited with depurative, astringent, invigorating and healing properties.

Sandalwood Oil

Credited with astringent, anti-inflammatory,

antibacterial, tonic, stimulant, cooling and soothing properties, beneficial in cases of curing acne and used as astringent for oily skin. The oil may produce rashes on hypersensitive skin, when present in high concentration.

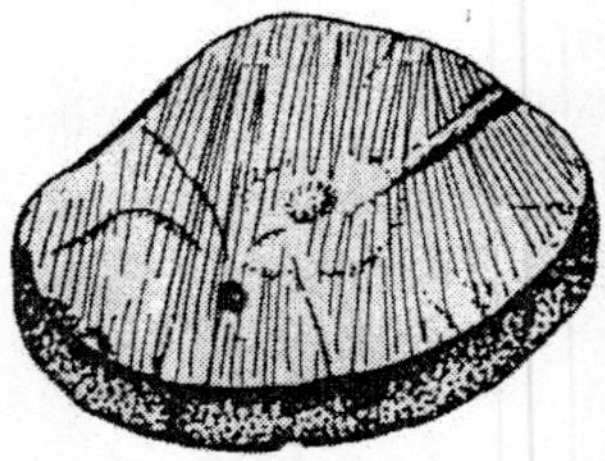

SANDAL WOOD

Sesame Oil

It is commonly used as a carrier oil for cosmetic products. It has emollient properties similar to nut and vegetable oil. Sesame oil derived from the seeds is useful is suntan lotions, and reduced the 30 percent of the sun's burning UV rays.

Shahtara (Pitpapda)

An herbal plant with fine leaves, found in wheat fields with bitter taste and violet flowers. It has been extensively used for disorders arising out of impurities in the blood, like scabies, ringworm besides curing venereal diseases such as Syphilis and gonorrhoea.

Sheesham (Red Wood)

The oil exuding from this plant is used for many disorders of the skin. It is used as a very efficacious blood purifier curing scabies, ringworm and leucoderma.

Satyanasi (pela-dhatura)

A medicinal plant with yellow flowers and thorny branches. Used as a blood purifier and cures many diseases of the skin. Powder of the seeds use to counteract the itch resulting from venereal diseases, cures scabies and destroys intestinal parasitis.

Sorbitol

Obtained from the leaves, absorb a moisture from the air, which helps to prevent skin dryness, leaves the skin feeling smooth and velvety is used as a replacement for glycerin in emulsions, ointments and various cosmetic creams.

Soapwort Extract (Saboonbooti)

It is credited with cleansing and soothing properties. It helps soothing to the skin and relieves itching and inflammation. Soapwort extract is used for treating acne, psoriasis and eczema. The main constituents of this extract made from the roots, leaves and stem include flavonoids and vitamin C, which leave a magic effect on the skin.

Speedwell

The herbal plant with oval-shaped leaves and pale-blue flowers, also known as veronica is prescribed in medicines for treating catarrh, bronchitis, asthama and digestive trouble. Used as a standard infusion internally as well as externally it treats most skin eruptions such as sores, ulcers, pimples, eczema and pruritus. Pure infusion can be applied as an eye lotion to improve the lesion in consultation with a Naturopath.

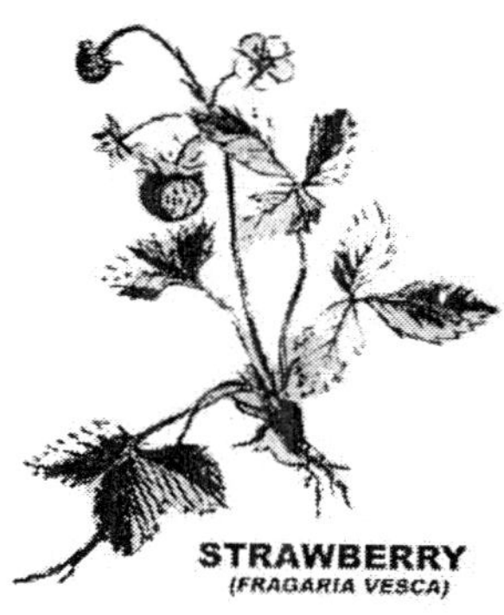

STRAWBERRY
(FRAGARIA VESCA)

Strawberry

It possesses considerable medical value as well as a remarkable cooling effecting on the skin and controls excessive perspiration. Having astringent properties, the herb is useful in dealing with diarrhoea, menstruation disorders, threatened abortion, risk of hemorrhage and the digestive system. Strawberry juice can be used to treat more serious skin ailments. It contains maximum iron contents and cures anaemia. It helps curing more serious skin ailments such as eczema, pruritus and sunburned skins.

Thyme (Ban Ajwain)

The herb grows wild on dry banks and heaths, has woody stems and flattish round leaves and heavily scented flowers. Thyme have cleansing properties and its poultice made from leaves combat inflammation and infection. Thyme is digestive, used as a liver tonic and cures a wide range of psychological disorders, headaches, histeria, halitosis and various female ailments. Thyme oil obtained from branches and flowers is considered a powerful product having botanical properties such as antiseptic, tonic, antibacterial, deodorizing, fungicidal and circulation stimulating. The oil is obtained from the herb's branches and flowers.

THYME

Tamarind (Imli)

Credited with astringent, antiseptic and strong immuno-stimulating properties. Constituents of this plant include citric, tartaric and malic acids, potassium bitartrate, polysaccharides, proteins and lipids. This botanical is recommended for protecting the skin against environmentally induced damage, stimulating skin repair and for skin with low immuno defenses.

Tea Tree Oil

A natural preservative with antiseptic, germicidal and expectorant properties. The oil cures fungus, skin disorders and infections of all type of skins. It exhibits positive benefits against seborrhea, psoriasis, scaling and redness of skin, eczema, itching and dermatitis and problem of congested skins.

Turmeric

Credited to healing, tonic, mildly stimulating, anti-inflammatory and blood-purifying properties. This herb is useful for a variety of curative purposes including the treatment of acne, eczema, skin infections, ulcers, burns and rashes.

Vervain

The plant having green-grey leaves and small hooded mauve flowers has properties to cure nervous disorders, epilepsy , asthama, forties the liver, heart and spleen. It relieves mental strain and helps cure infectious diseases, used as gargle or mouthwash for sore throats and gums and as an eye lotion. It is also recommended for curing inflammation and diseases of skin.

Walnut

The extract obtained from leaves and bark of the plant is traditionally used topically soothing and anti-itching, as well as against sunburns and other superficial burns. It can be used in case of acne and other skin diseases because of its fungistatic and astringent properties.

Witch Hazel (Hamamelis, winterbloom)

Traditionally used in topical treatment of burns, sunburns, skin irritation, insect bites and bruises. It is credited with anti-inflammatory and wound-healing properties, is used for anti-itching, softening and emollient properties.

Yarrow (Sahastrapani, Gandana)

Having greyish, feathery, ethereal-looking leaves and small daisy-like flowers, yarrow has been used for headaches, fevers (influenza), to curb diarrhoea, paltipations and excessive menstruation. The extract have astringent, antiseptic, anti-inflammatory, healing and calming properties. The important constituents include flavonoid, amino acids, sugars and phytosterols. It is beneficial for oily and acne skins.

Cactus Extract

An emulsifier for creams and lotions described as good for sunburns and other minor burns, insect bites, skin irritations, swelling and inflammatoins. It is used for face masks.

2

Your Ayurvedic Cosmetic Laboratory

Cosmetic Use of Herbs

For those in search of beauty and lost youth, herbs have always has held a special fascination, and one that our modern cosmetic industry have exploited. For this reason the cosmetic use of herbs is a subject to those intent on finding beauty. To maintain youth or beauty, people spend a lot, some on surgeons to stitch up double chins or de-bag eyes, others on expensive creams to banish acne and wrinkles. And despite all this, everybody ages and nothing can do stop it. Where certain herbs can help, perhaps, is in improving the faces we were born with and, where possible, delaying the more obvious marks of ageing. In other words, herbs will not create youth a beauty, but will enable us to make the most of what we have of either. An early experimenter in the field of herbal cosmetics was the Greek physician Galen who invented cold cream. He hit upon the idea of melting together white wax and oil of roses in a particular ratio, and then stirring into this mixture a cupful of water laced with spirit vinegar. Since Galen's time the oil of roses has been replaced by almond oil or even liquid paraffin, although the best substitute is sunflower oil particularly rich in vitamin A and vitamin D.

Making Your Own Cosmetics

Make good use of all kinds of everyday items like fruit, vegetables, nuts; cereals in nurturing their beauty. Even in most beauty conscious there is a definite tendency towards natural therapies. The kitchen larder is a store house of beauty aids. You just have to follow a few recipes, pick the ingredients, mix them in a required ratio and you will soon have a beauty lotion or cream in hand. These home-made herbal preparations help enhance beauty of the skin and complexion and delay ageing without causing harm. Taking care of your skin is a must in order to remain young. During youth the skin is elastic and smooth but as one grows older, the skin loses its elasticity, natural oils and water content. In days gone by, there were hardly any cosmetics available in the market and rural areas, and home made preparations were used for skin care. Since ancient times vegetable oils, refined animal fats and cream of milk have been used for the care of the skin and beauty. A number of costly modern creams available in the market today are still based on refined animal fat. These help in keeping the skin smooth.

Making your own creams, lotions is easy. By learning to make your own cosmetics, you cosmetics, you have at your fingertips not only more luxurious products than you could afford to buy but also those especially suitable for your skin. Most of the recipes mentioned in this book have been tested and are extremely easy to make. Creams and emulsions are all basically a mixture of water and oily substances, waxes and fragrances in varying proportions. A slight change in proportion change the character of the preparation. Be careful when measuring the ingredients. When measuring the quantity the following rough equivalents should be kept in mind:

60 drops	= 1 teaspoon (tps)		= 5 ml
3 teaspoons	= 1 tablespoon (tsp)		= 15 ml
2 tablespoon	= 1/8 cup or 16 table spoons		= 1 cup

Some Dos and Dont's : The following dos and don'ts should be kept in mind when making a herbal preparation at home:

- Do not expose oils and waxes to direct heat as these can burn and an intense heat can change the properties of the preparation.
- When heating oils and waxes, put them in separate enamel bowls, placed in a large pan filled with hot water (not boiling) and continue stirring with either a wooden spoon or a glass rod or a slow speed electric heater. While stirring, add water to the wax or the oils if it is too thick.
- Add perfume or colouring matter when the preparation is ready and in case of a cream, mix it when it cools and thickens. In case your skin is sensitive or allergy-prone, it is advised to omit perfume.
- Ensure that the contents of the preparation are properly mixed otherwise preparation may turn gritty. Make sure to continue Stirring or beating until the cream is cool. If the preparation does not gel, melt it again and repeat the process. You may add a few drops of oleic acid to bind together any cream or lotion.
- The herbal ingredients used in preparing the cosmetics may be easily available with leading 'pansari' shops or a herbal store or dispensing chemists.

- Bees wax, emulsifying wax and cocoa butter can be available with a dispensing chemist. Lanolin is readily available with the chemists. These are usually of two types- anhydrous and hydrous. Anhydrous lanolin is commonly used because it has less water contents. In case, anhydrous lanolin is not readily available, you may procure hydrous lanolin, which has in itself a fairly large water contents. The preparations with anhydrous lanolin will be much more richer and greasier. Oils, herbs, lentils, fuller's earths, camphor, etc. can be purchased from a 'pansari' shop or a good herbal store.
- Home made herbal cosmetic preparations have a short life, which can be lengthened by storing them in a refrigerator. It is suggested to make a small quantity of the recipe and use them lavishly while still fresh. Keep a small jar in the bathroom and the rest in the refrigerator. Nepagin M is an effective preservative. When heating the contents, add a few drops of Nepagin M. Stir constantly until the oily globules disperse. This will enhance the shelf life of preparation.

Fruits, vegetable and natural substances: Here is a brief description of some of the very useful ingredients required in making Ayurvedic preparations for health and beauty:

Amla (Emblice myrobalan)

Cheapest source of vitamin C which is not destroyed by boiling or other process. A good substance for hair washing and helps in case of falling and premature graying of hair. It rejuvenates the body.

Anar (Pomegranate)

A delicious juicy fruit with many medicinal

properties, It is cooling and allays uncontrollable thirst in diarrhoea, digestive. Flowers of the plant are an ingredient for miscarriage. The rind of fruit is an astringent and have a tonic effect on the tissues. Bark of root of the plant is used in case of intestinal worms.

Alcohol

It has antiseptic, preserving and grease cutting properties. Used mainly in stimulating astringents and as a solvent for essential oils. Vodka is a common substitute for alcohol.

Arand Kharbuza

Also called as golden tree of life which acts as a digestive agent because of large amounts of pepsin. It is used to reduce inflammation of live and spleen. The sap of tree cures ringworm and intestinal parasites.

Alum

A fine white or yellow powder with astringent properties, also knows as 'fitkari'. It is used in lotions and as dry shampoo to remove sweat and dirt.

Apple

A naturally acid fruit good for the skin. Apple cider restores the acid mantle to the skin. Can be used as skin tonic.

Apricot (Khubani)

Rich in vitamin A. Use the pulp in face masks. Apricot oil is very rich in polyunsaturated oil, so it is used in nourishing creams.

Banana

Nourishing and used in masks.

Beeswax

Also known as 'madhu-mom'. It is an easter wax with a high melting point, ideal for face creams. An emulsifier when mixed with borax. It takes eight parts of honey to produce one part of beeswax. It is one of the oldest raw ingredients used in cosmetic preparations, Beeswax is used as part of the wax composition of solid and paste products such as creams, lipstick and pomades. Beeswax is credited with antiinflammatory, antiallergic, antioxidant, anti-bactericidal, germicidal, skin softening and elasticity enhancing properties. It rarely causes sensitivity, and allergic reaction. Bleached beeswax is white whereas unbleached beeswax is yellow.

Beer

Used to wash the face and as a hair setting lotion. It prevents skin rashes.

Barley

It has nutritional value and is rich in iron and vitamin B. It cools the body, strengthens the nerves, and is excellent tonic food during convalescence.

BARLEY

Basil (Tulsi)

Has blood purifying qualities. It is used for ringworm, scabies, leucoderma and even leprosy.

Benzoin

A fragrant essential oil with bactericidal, anti-irritation and anti-itching properties. It is considered a good ingredient for reducing skin redness and is also a preservative of fats. While its primary constituents is benzoic acid, it also contains canaline and an oily aromatic liquid. Also known as 'lohban'.

Borax (Suhaga)

It has mild detergent and anti-septic properties. Used as emulsifier in conjuction with beeswax. It cures the patient of ringworm.

Bade (Banyan tree)

It is also known as Bodhi tree. It has many medicine properties to prepare formulations for spermatorrhoe, premature ejaculation etc. Sap of its leaves is specific for kibes and corns.

Bakain (Lilac)

A tree resembling neem. The leaves have blood purifying properties; recommended for scabies, ringworm, leprosy, leucoderma and to reduce inflammation.

Calamine Lotion

An alkaline lotion used to soothe irritated skin. It contains lime water, glycerine, zinc oxide and calamine.

Camphor

A white crystalline substance used as an antiseptic. It is healing and soothing when used on spot. It is used either camphor cake or camphor spirit. Camphor oil is stimulating.

Castor Oil (arandi ka tel)

A rich oil used in hair products. Leaves of the tree smeared with sesame oil and applied to inflammations tend to relieve them. It has many medicine used also.

Carrot Juice (gajar ka ras)

Rich in vitamin A, B and C. Used in nourishing eye creames. Carrot oil have cleansing, depurative and draining properties and cures acne, dermatitis, wrinkles and skin irritation.

Cocoa Butter

Solidified waxy oil from the roasted cocoa beans, used as lubricant in massage creames. It is good for dry skins.

Corn Oil (gram seed oil)

A heavy vegetable oil which can be used in body and face creams .

Coconut oil

Used as a cream base. A raw material in soaps, ointments, massage creams and in sunscreen formulations. Coconut oil is a grouping of primarily short-chain fatty acid bonded with glycerine and expressed from coconut kernels . It may be irritating to the skin and cause skin rashes .

Caraway oil (carum carvi)

A carrier oil having ability to remove bruises, and believed to have tissue regenerating properties . It is beneficial for acne or an oily skin .

Citric oils

Refers to one or a combination of oil from citrus fruits such as orange oil, lemon oil, grapefruit oil and the like.

Corn oil

Used as a carrier oil. This vegetable oil has average

emollient properties. It is widely used in cosmetic formulations.

Cotton seed oil

The oil is used in the manufacture of soaps, creams and baby creams. It is known to cause allergies and be mildly irritating. Expressed from various species of cotton.

Cucumber

It is slightly astringent, cool and refreshing, and used in lotions, creams and masks.

Fuller's Earth (multani mitti)

An absorbent clay, rich in minerals. Used in face masks for thickening and cleansing, drawing and stimulating qualities. Also used as dry shampoo. A paste on the skin cures prickely heat.

Cucumber extract

Credited with moisture-binding, moisture-regulating, soothing, tightening, anti-itching, refreshing, softening, healing and antiinflammatory properties. It contains amino acids and organic acids that are claimed to strengthen the skin's acid mantle. The extract can be used in aftershave preparations, eye treatment products and treatment for oily skin. It is also effective in emulsions as a tightening agent for, stressed skin and in suntan preparations as a refresher.

Eggs

The most useful aid to beauty. The yolk is nourishing and the white is drying and tightening. Used in masks and as a hair conditioner. Egg protein creates a film, thereby acting as a moisture-retention agent allowing the skin to build up a supply of water. The moisturizing process tightens and softens the skin only temporarily as the skin cannot utilize the protein contained in a egg. It may cause skin rashes and other disorders in those with an allergy to eggs. Egg lecithin is recommended for sensitive skins. The egg oil extracted form the egg yolk is recommended for sensitive skins. The egg yolk extract is a protein with emulsifying capabilities, contains lecithin sterols and vitamin A.

Emulsifying wax

Extremely useful for stabilizing creams. Made from ceto stearyl alcohol and sodium lauryl sulphate. It is an emulsifier and thickening agent used to give body to a formulation. Unlike some waxes including beeswax, this is not a true wax. It is a chemical mixture of emulsifiers and fatty alcohols that permit the formulation of stable creams.

Glycerin

Attracts and holds moisture. Used in face creams and lotions. Glycerin is used in moisturizers due to its water-binding capabilities that absorb water from the air. Glycerin helps the skin retain moisture. Glycerin also improves the spreading qualities of creams and lotions. It is clear syrupy liquid made by chemically combining water and fat that is usually derived from vegetable oil.

Gelatine

A rich source of protein used for hair conditioning or diluted as a setting lotion and nail hardening cream.

Glucose

Has moisture-binding properties and provides the

skin with a soothing effect. It is a sugar that is generally obtained by the hydrolysis of starch.

Grapes

Slightly acid and good for cleansing and bleaching. It is described as tonic, with antiinflammatory and decongestant properties. It may act as an antioxidant. Grapes are beneficial in anti-aging, after-sun and other sun care products. Grape seed oil has moisturizing and nourishing properties due to its high linoleic acid content.

Groundnut oil

A vegetable oil used in face creams and body lotions. Also known as peanut oil.

Gum Resin

Used as a tightening, fixing and stabilizing agent in the cream. It can be dissolved in water.

Honey

Healing, nourishing and softening. It is used in masks, cream and lotions. A perfect food if taken with milk or lime water. It is helpful in cases of paralysis and cures suppurating (pussy) wounds and improve eyesight.

Hydrogen peroxide

A bleaching and oxidizing agent, detergent and antiseptic. A skin bleacher in cosmetics. If used undiluted, it can cause burns of the skin and mucous membranes.

Hydrolyzed milk protein

Forms a film on the skin's surface that allows the skin to retain moisture.

Kaolin (China Clay)

Oftenly used in powders and masks. It is appropriate absorber of the oil and sweat secreted by the skin.

Lanolin

A thick tacky fat, widely used in skin foods for its moisturizing and softening effects. Lanolin is an emollient with moisturizing properties and an emulsifier with high water- absorption capabilities.

Linseed oil

Botanical properties are listed as emollient, antiinflammatory, and healing. Derived from the flax plant seed obtained by expression with little or no heat.

Lovage oil

A scribed botanical properties such as cleansing, depurative, and draining make lovage oil appropriate for use on oily skin.

Lecithin Powder

A complex, highly nutritious soft yellow powder found in egg yolk and soyabeans. It is an natural emollient, emulsifier, antioxidant, and spraying agent that attracts water and acts as a moisturizer.

Neem (Margosa Tree)

Bitter leaves used as an antiseptic. Neem leaves when ground in paste and applied relieve prickly heat, remove pus from wounds, clean boils on the skin. All parts of the tree are endowed with the quality of purifying blood.

Melon

Used on dry skin for refreshing and cleaning the skin.

Mint (Pudina)

Extensively used in cooking, has great digestive properties. It cures acne, blemishes and is and varicose veins.

Milk

Used for softening, nourishing and cleaning the skin. Milk cream gives a smooth feel to the skin.

Milk protein, primarily is well absorbed by the skin and gives a it gloss and fine touch by forming a soft film.

Oatmeal (jai ka atta)

A cleansing and soothing meal. Use it for washing with, or in masks. Finally ground oat-meal is found in any grocer's shop.

Oak

Oak leaves in the bath are deodorant and relaxing. They soothe inflammation.

Onion

An antiseptic. Wash your face with onion juice to prevent blemishes and mix it with honey to make an anti-wrinkle cream. Juice of onion taken in conjunction with honey and eggs, it is an excellent tonic with aphrodisiac qualities. An excellent preparation against cholera and diarrhoea if steeped in vinegar.

Orange

Contains vitamin C. The juice is used in skin tonics and masks. Dry and grind some orange peel and use it in masks and facial scrubs. Also used in tooth powders.

Olive oil

A poly-unsaturated vegetable oil used in nourishing creams. Olive oil is a carrier oil with excellent lubricity, pale colour, and low odour. Olive oil is considered an especially good carrier for essential oils.

Papaya

It is also called paw-paw. Softening and cleansing. The enzymes in the fruit have a deep cleansing effect by breaking down the dead cells of the skin. It contains Calcium, Iron, Phosphorus and Magnesium salt.

Peach

Moisturizing, nourishing and delicious smelling. Use the mashed pulp on dry, rough skin in skin tonics and masks.

Petroleum Jelly

A lubricating jelly often used in cleansing creams, and hand and nail creams.

Paraffin

Used in cosmetics as a beeswax substitute. Paraffin is a solid mixture of hydrocarbons obtained from petroleum. Presence of impurities in paraffin may result in irritation, eczema and other skin problems.

Panwar (Mihndi)

A herb growing in waste lands. Has seeds like kidney beans. Ground seed applied to skin cures ringworm, leucoderma and blemishes.

Palmitic Acid

Obtained from palm oil, one of the skin's major fatty acids produced by the sebaceous glands. In cosmetic preparations, it is used as a formula texturizer.

Peanut Oil

Utilized as a skin softener, emulsifier and emollient. It is used as a substitute for expensive oils such as almond and olive in cosmetic creams. Peanut oil has a higher vitamin A, vitamin E and nicotinic acid content than other nut oils. Potatoes

Have cleansing and drawing properties. Clears the skin. Use thin raw potato slices for eye pads to remove puffiness of eyes.

Resin

Used to give gloss, flow, adhesion and water resistance to cosmetics. This is a brittle substance, usually translucent or transparent, that can be either derived naturally or synthetically obtained.

Retinol

Considered a skin revitalizer, retinol is reported to enhance skin radiance and treat conditions associated with aging such as wrinkles and fine lines, as well as dermatological disorders including acne, and lesion papules.

Safflower Oil

A rich poly-unsaturated oil suitable for all nourishing cosmetics. A carrier oil considered hydrating to the skin, is obtained from the seeds and have astringent, anti-inflammatory and soothing properties especially for sensitive skin and areas with burns.

St. John's wort oil (Basant)

Considered antiinflammatory. It is beneficial for sensitive and/or rough, chapped skin as well as skins suffering from acne, irritation and inflammatory circulation.

Sodium Chloride (Salt)

Used as a preservative, astringent and antiseptic to treat inflame lesions. Sodium sisqui is a powdery substance which is a water softener and is used in bath salts. Salt is used with equal parts of bicarbonate of soda as an excellent tooth powder. Also used as an abrasive body rub to tone the skin and improve circulation.

Sodium Bicarbonate (baking soda)

An inorganic salt used as a buffering agent and a pH adjuster. Used in skin smoothing powders and also serves as a neutralizer.

Sodium Bisulphate

An organic salt used as an buffering agent and a pH adjuster in cosmetic creams.

Sarson (Mustard)

A well known oil seed. The seeds of the plant used for extracting oil used for massage, as cooking medium and also as hair oil.

Stearic Acid

A natural fatty acid. It is crystalline, white, waxy substance, which gives pearliness to creams, hand and body lotions.

Sugar

An abrasive face scrub. Lather the face with soap, then add a handful of sugar and scrub, rinse off and apply lemon juice. This thoroughly cleanses and stimulates the skin.

Sulphur

A yellow powder used in acne preparations. It helps slow down the activity of the oil producing glands. Some people are allergic to it, so before using it on your face, give yourself a skin test behind the ear.

Tea

Contains tannin which has a soothing and healing effect. It absorbs ultraviolet light and is used in sun creams to help prevent burning. Tea bags are marvellously soothing ready made eye pads.

Soybean Oil

Used as a smoothing ingredient. It has high content of phosphatides such as lecithin, sterols and vitamins (A,E, and K). Soybean oil is not irritating.

Spermaceti

A waxy substance used in the manufacture of cosmetics, to thicken the products and give them shine. Spermaceti is non-toxic and non-irritating.

Tamanu Oil

Used for the improvement of cell regeneration. It can be found in products used to protect the skin against sun exposure, as well as anti-aging formulations to cure wrinkles.

Tomato

A slightly acidic vegetable containing potassium and vitamin C. Use it on blackheads, open pores and greasy skin.

Turtle Oil

Vitamin enriched oil. Often used in rich nourishing creams. Very effective but smells bad.

Vinegar

Acidic. Use diluted eight parts water to one part vinegar. Improves and softens the skin.

Vetiver Oil (Khus-Khus)

Produced from the roots of a fragrant grass. Considered stimulant and tonic, and used in perfumery as well as in cosmetics.

Vervain Oil

Has been credited with astringent and anti-spasmodic properties.

Vitamins

Valuable for skin and hair. Vitamin A can pass through the skin and is useful for dry skin and acne. Also have soothing properties. Vitamin B promotes health of skin and hair. Vitamin C promotes healing of acne. Vitamin D can be absorbed through skin and has a healing effect on the skin. Vitamin E is said to have healing properties. Vitamin F counteracts dry, chapped skin. Greatly used in face and hand creams, and in hair treatments to counter act brittle hair.

Wheatgerm Oil

Made from twigs of hamamelis or alder bush. Widely used in skin tonics for its astringent properties. Traditionally used in topical treatment of burns, sunburns, skin irritation, insect bites and bruises. It is credited with antiinflammatory and wound healing properties. It is used for its ant-itching, softening and emollient properties.

Yoghurt

A liquor made from milk. It contains enzymes. Used as a base for cleansing and cleaning face masks.

3

Ayurveda for Digestive Disorders

Ayurveda consists of two words : 'Ayu' and 'Veda'. In Sanskrit term it means the science of life - also called Science of living. It not only deals with the prevention of diseases and maintain good health but it also cures diseases - even chronic disorders. According to the Shastras the knowledge of Ayurveda was given to Daksha Prajapati by Brahma - the creator of the universe. Ayurveda has eight branches: **Kayachikitsa (general medicine), Shalya (surgery), Shalakya (treatment of disease of head, neck, eye, nose and throat), Gralia chikitsa (psychotherapy), Damstra chikitsa (toxicology), Bala Roga chikitsa (paediatrics), Jara chikitsa (rejuvenating) and Vrishya chikitsa (aphrodisics).** The universe has five basic elements : Prithvi (earth), Ap (water), Tejo (fire), Vayu (air) and Akasha (ether).

According to Indian philosophy and Ayurveda, the human body is made up of above substances - thus there is natural harmony between the universe and human being. Ayurveda believes in the theory of Tridosha: Vata, Pitta and Kapha. Vata is a powerful force in the body produced by Vayu and Akasha Bhootas. Kapha is produced due to the predominance of Prithvi and Abhootas Bhootas (earth and water). Pitta is produced due to predominance of Tejas. According to Ayurveda, the disease is produced mainly due to the imbalance of tridoshas and the regimen of diet is more important than medicine, and there is no need for medicine if one takes proper food. Diet plays an important role in regulating the health of an individual. Health controls the functioning and equilibrium of the body, mind and soul.

The normal Vata is of five kinds such as Prana (source of life), Udana (source for the strength of the body and mind), Vyana (nourishes the entire system of body through blood and secretion of perspiration), Samana (moves all over alimentary tract and controls the digestion fire and enzymes) and Apana (helps in expulsion of urine, faeces, flatus and foetus, menstruation and semen). There are five types of Pitta such as Panchaka (responsible for digestion of food), Ranjaka (gives colour to the food / juice from stomach to the liver), Sadhaka (helps in the normal functioning of the mind and its activities), Bhrajaka (regulates the tint of the skin) and Alochaka (regulates vision), Lika Vata and Pitta, the Kapha also have five types such as Kledaka (helps in moistening the food in stomach), Avalambaka (protects the heart from excessive heat or cooling effect), Bhodhaka (aid in detecting taste of food and helps in increasing appetite), Tarpaka (cools the eyes and nose) and Sleshaka (helps proper functioning of joints of the body).

In addition to Vata, Pitta and Kapha, Ayurveda gives importance to another element - **'Agni'**, which is called Pitta (panchaka pitta). Its function is to digest the food and promote health. There are 13 types of Agnis in the body of which 7 are Dhatvagnis (enzymes), 5 Bhootagnis and 1 Jatharagni (digestive fire in the stomach). Human body has 7 Dhatus such as Rasa (chyle), Raka (Blood), Mamsa (Flesh), Meda (Fat), Asthi (Bones), Majja (Bone narrow) and Shukra (Semen). The Ayurvedic line of treatment aims at the removal of doshas from the body and most of the diseases are produced due to 'ama' (uncooked or undigested material) - usually said to be indigestion which acts as a toxin or allergen which spread in the body through the blood and other fluids. To eradicate these toxins 'Malas' (secretions) play an important role. The important 'malas' are Mala (faeces), Mootra (urine) and sweda (sweat).

A healthy body is beautiful. A fat surplus of 8 to 15 per cent, over the normal weight, must be considered as overweight. Beyond that, it is obesity. Over 30 per cent, it is extreme obesity. Heredity factor, habit of overeating, poor functioning of the digestive system, nervous factor, sedentary life cause constipation and overweight. There are three categories of overweight: fatty overweight, watery overweight and cellulitis. Fatty overweight is really 'fat and muscle' uniformly spread and is more usual in men. It is often more noticeable over the upper part of the body - head, neck, arms and trunk. Watery overweight does not affect the muscles; is most usual over the lower half of the body and is common among women. Cellulitis is a form of infiltration rather than overweight.

The warning signals of overweight include when the skirt belt or jean gets a little tight, there is strain on jacket buttons, the face start growing round, the skin gets puffy and the skin loses its firm and taut, shoulders get plump and the hollows over the collarbones, fat overhangs the hips and the waist disappears, the buttocks enlarge, the girdle squeezes the flesh and swell out above and below it, the neck thickens and lose its normal contour, a double chin under the nape of the neck follows, breasts sag down to the stomach, the stomach droops over the pubis and the pubis swells modestly over the genital organs. Being overweight not only affects one's looks and figure, but also damages one's health.

The obese persons with slight exertion, get paltipations, experience pain in the heart and the heart gets tired resulting in heart troubles. There is always a possibility of high blood pressure and diabetes or gout (gathia). An obese person is affected by psychological and nervous troubles which cause irritation, tiredness, nervousness, athetic and lethargic atmosphere. Overweight cause digestive problems such as dilation of stomach, inflammation, spasma of intestines, congestion of liver and digestive upsets. It gives rise to genital disorders due to the infiltration of fat into the nervous and glandular tissues which control sexual appetite and cause impotence. Girls between the age of 14 and 18 tend to put on excess weight, largely because their bodies are undergoing natural changes around this time. It becomes a real mental burden for those afflicted with it. Even if the problem does not cause danger to physical health, its psychological effect can be far more damaging. To maintain a perfect figure, the amount of energy you consume must be equal to the amount of energy you burn. There is a difference between obesity and overweight. Overweight is not obesity, but every obese person is overweight. It has been observed that an obese person loses average two to three kgs of weight every month to fight obesity practising a few exercises supported by a balanced diet.

Calories are energy units, and all foods contain calories to a greater or lesser degree. A normal everyday diet of a woman who is not pregnant or not engaged in physical labour requires 2200 to 2300 calories daily to fulfil the needs. A normal healthy male person needs approx. 2500 calories in a day . Protein intake should account for about 50 per cent of daily calories consumption. Starchy and foods containing sugar should be minimised as much as possible in favour of protein-rich foods. Normally, a healthy body digests the food within 15 to 20 minutes and converts it into energy. One gram protein or carbohydrate gives four calories whereas One gram of fat gives nine calories. Milk, eggs, meat and fish, soyabean, almond, coconut, groundnut etc are rich sources of protein and give strength to the body. Deficiency of carbohydrates leads to weakness.

Ayurveda believes that disease is an abnormal condition of the body resulting from the violation of the natural laws which adversely affect the human system in the shape of lowered vitality, irregularities of the blood and lymph and the accumulation of waste matter and toxins. When toxins accumulate, organs such as the bowels, kidneys, skin and lungs are worst affected. The first and most basic principle of Ayurveda is the accumulation of waste materials in the system which steadily pile up in the body through faulty living habits, improper body care, worry and overwork. The only way to cure disease is to employ methods which enable the system to throw off these toxic accumulations. Another principle of Ayurveda is that the body contains an elaborate healing mechanism which has the power to bring about a normal condition of health. The power to cure diseases lies within the body itself and not in the hands of the doctor. The modern medical system treats the symptoms and suppresses the disease but does little to ascertain the real cause, Toxic drugs, may suppress or relieve ailments, usually have harmful side-effects. When drugs are used, the patient has to recover twice-once from the illness, and once from the drug. An important factor in the cure of diseases by natural methods is to stimulate the vitality of the body with the help of packs and cold hip bath, especially to the abdomen, the seat of most diseases, and to the sexual organs which lower body heat and stimulate the nervous system. Other Ayurvedic methods useful in the cure of diseases are air and sun baths to revive dead skin, exercise and massage to tone up the nervous system and stimulate blood circulation, eliminate mental tension (physical, mental and emotional), a well balanced diet, fresh air, plenty of sunlight, pure drinking water, scrupulous cleanliness, adequate rest and right mental attitude.

RECOMMENDED DIETARY ALLOWANCE (RDA)

An woman should consume approximately 1900 to 2200 and men approx 2200 to 2500 Kcal/day as daily energy requirement. However, during pregnancy and breast feeding energy requirements are higher and a woman needs between 2200 to 2500 Kcal/day. These requirements should be supplemented by a balanced combination of carbohydrates , protein, vegetables and fat moderation. The keyword here is quality and not quantity. It's not about how much you eat, but what you eat. All food groups provide energy, which is expressed in technical terms as kilocalories (kcal). You need to provide your body with 2200 to 2500 kcal of Energy per day. Protein (65 gm/day) is required for a good overall growth and development. Pulses, dairy products, soyabean are excellent source of vegetarian protein. Calcium (1000 mg/day) is required for the development of bones and teeth. Dairy products, soyabean products, green leafy vegetables and sesame seeds are loaded with calcium. Iron (40mg/day) is an essential component of haemoglobin that supplies oxygen to each cell of the human body, especially red blood cell production. Foods with high iron sources are dried beans , cereals and pulses, dried fruits, green leafy vegetables, nuts and jaggery. Folic acid (400 mcg/day) is an essential vitamin required especially for women going to conceive and also during the early stage of pregnancy for the growth and development of the foetus and breast feeding. Its deficiency leads to anaemia. Potatoes, vegetables, cereals and pulses, soyabean, are rich source of Folic Acid. Fat (30 gms Per/day) is essential to enhance energy. Vitamin C (40 mg/day) is necessary to fight against infections and diseases. It provides structure to the bones, cartilage, muscles and blood vessels. Citrus fruits, amla, vegetables and fruits boost up with plenty of vitamin C. Vitamin A (Beta-Carotene 2400 mcg/day) is required for clear vision and healthy skin. Vitamin A level can be maintained with orange, vegetables (carrot and pumpkin), fruits (mango, papaya and tomatoes), green leafy vegetables and whole milk. Vitamin D is synthesized through sunlight which aids the absorption of calcium in the body. The quantity and quality of milk produced in the breasts is not related to the size of breast but is dependent on the amount of fluids a feeding mother consume. A feeding mother should drink plenty of juices, milk shakes, buttermilk, soups, water etc. and have at least 4 litres of fluid per day. The nutritional quality of breast milk is much higher than that of cow's milk or buffalo's milk as it contains vitamins A , C and E.

Juice Therapy

It is also known as juice fasting and is most effective way to restore health and rejuvenate the body. Raw juice therapy is an exclusive diet of juices of fruits and vegetables which results in much faster and effective recovery from diseases which cleanse and regenerate the tissues than the fasting. Drinking alkali-forming fruit and vegetable juices, during fasting increase the healing effect of fasting. All juices should be made fresh immediately before drinking. A glass of water mixed with lemon juice and 20 to 30 grams of honey may be taken first in the morning. Thereafter, the prescribed juice may be taken at three-hourly intervals. The patient should take adequate rest during the raw juice therapy.

Juice of grapes helps in case of acidity, acne and pimples, skin allegries, anaemia, constipation, insominia, hypertension, heart disease, jaundice, liver ailments, menstruation disorders, psoriasis, stomach ulcer, sore throat and varicose veins. **Orange juice** helps curing acidity, cold, hypertension, kidney disorders, neuritis, piles, obesity and verciose veins. **Apple Juice** is good for recovery of constipation, colitis, halitosis, bladder infection, kidney troubles and neuritis. **Pineapple juice** benefits arthritis, colitis, gout, halitosis, sore throat, neuritis, diarrhoea, obesity and tonsilitis. **Juice of apricot** helps curing skin allergies, anaemia, asthama, bronchitis, diarrhoea, insomnia, liver ailments, headache, jaundice, pils, obesity, sore throat and rheumatism. **Carrot juice** helps in curing acidity, acne and pimples on the face, skin allergies, anaemia, arthritis, colitis, diabetes, epilepsy, eczema, jaundice, insomina, hypertension, heart disease, headache, halitosis, liver ailments, sinus trouble and tonsilitis. **Spinach Juice** helps to cure acidity, acne and pimples, constipation, colitis, eczema, eye disorders, heart disease, jaundice, prostrate, and rheumatism. **Juice of Lettuce** cures arthritis, diabetes, headache, insomnia, menstruation problems and prostrates. **Tomato juice** helps ot cure acne/pimples, bronchitis, eye disorder, halitosis, liver ailments, gout and rheumatism. **Cucumber Juice** helps in curing acne/pimples, arthritis, bladder malfunctioning, eczema, gout, jaundice, liver ailments and psoriasis. The juice of **Potato** cures acne and pimples where as **Onion juice** relieves bronchitis, cold and sinus trouble.

AYURVEDIC REMEDIES FOR DISEASES OF DIGESTIVE SYSTEM

Some of the common disorders include indigestion, constipation, diarrhoea, dysentry, dyspepsia, ulcer of the stomach, jaundice, colic gastralgia, intestinal parasites, ageusia (loss of sense of taste), anorexia (loss of appetite) excessive thirst, nausea and vomiting. **Constipation** may be defined as infrequent bowel evacuation or decreased frequency of usual bowel movements. If the stool are unusually hard, dry and difficult to expel, the patient is said to be constipated. The main causes include habitual or due to certain diseases. Addiction to tea, coffee and smoking, excessive use of laxatives and purgatives, stress, sluggish peristalsis in old age, change of place of evacuation (pscyhogenic), lack of exercise, erratic and poor diet, insffucient food and water intake, use of drugs are habitual causes whereas obstructive colonic disorders (Carcinoma of rectum, colon and congenital megacolon), absence of autonomic nerve plexus in a segment of colon, intestinal obstruction due to round worms in children, T.B. of abdomen, Weakness of intestinal system and abdominal muscles are due to diseases. Constipation is a condition in which the bowels are evacuated at a longer interval with difficulty. **Signs and Symptoms** include cracked tongue, loss of appetite, headache and discomfort, abdominal pain, flatulence in abdomen and other complications such as piles and ulcer. The treatment suggested include a correct diet therapy such as adequate food in take, consumption of food having high fibre content (bran, raw fruits and vegetables) and adequate fluids. Drink atleast eight glasses of water a day. **Exercises** relieve constipation and improve digestive system. Hip bath should be given regularly followed by abdominal massage. A fomentation should be administered. Change of food habits; milk, boiled vegetables" fruit and fruit juices should be taken in excess quantity.

Ayurvedic Remedies:

Eat 2 tsp. Gulkand (confection of rose petals) with milk. Another way is to steep 2 tsp. pulp of purging cassia (amaltas) in water overnight, strain in the morning and drink mixing to it 1 tsp. sugar. Ajmoda seeds (two parts) mixed to one part Aniseed (saunf) and sugar taken twice daily is a beneficial remedy. Alternatively the powder of ginger, black pepper, mint (pudina) and celery seeds (ajamoda) taken in the morning and evening leave a curative effect. Rose petal jelly is a useful Ayurvedic remedy for constipation. To make it mix 1 tbs. lemon juice, 2 tbs. orange juice, 2 tbs clear honey, 400 gm white cane sugar and 150 ml water. Stir until the sugar dissolves. Add to it 100 gm white rose petal and heat gently until the petals appear to dissolve. Allow the mixture to cool stirring constantly, you will have syrup with transparent pieces of petal floating in it. In case of a child dilute a few drops of any essential oil (Rosemary, Hyssop, Fennel, Majoram or Camomile) with sunflower or olive oil and soothe wretched tummy giving a gentle rubbing to relieve tension and encourage bowel movement.

Fasting

is used to cleanse the body of all the imbedded waste matter, remove the deep rooted toxins and give rest to the different organs of the body. In order to prepare the body for fasting begin with eating only raw vegetables for 4-5 days. For the next four days take only liquid diet including the juice of raw vegetables or fruits. Do not consume more than 4-5 glasses of liquid a day. Now you are ready for complete fasting. Take only fresh lime with honey or plain water for next four to seven days. Just like you cannot begin fasting suddenly you cannot end it suddenly. So for the next four days take only raw or boiled vegetables. And slowly, over a period of ten days, you can come back to your original cereal diet. Many of the ailments e.g. acne, rheumtism, asthma, ulcers, alcoholism, heart disease and many other diseases just seem to dissolve while fasting.

Indigestion

Pain in the stomach, heart burn, tenderness over the stomach, badly coated tongue, acidity or belching of gas, headache, vomiting and pain in the back are common symptoms of chronic indigestion. These are caused due to eating too fast, partially cooked foods habit, use of intoxicant liquors, indulging in desk work, untimely meals, eating between meals, late hour eating, emotional upsets, severe mental strain and constipation generally cause indigestion. The treatment include eating well balanced, well cooked, well chewed food. Do not over eat. Eat only when you are hungry. Never eat when you are tired, emotionally upset and anxious. Enema should be given at the time of commencement of the treatment to clean bowels. Hot fomentation, mud pack on abdomen daily, cold hip bath twice a day, oil massage and mud bath are beneficial in curing indigestion and dyspepsia. Avoid taking seeds, fried food, spiced foods, processed foods and sour things. Dyspepsia is nothing but indigestion when the patient experiences pain in stomach flatulence, belching, sour taste in the mouth and heart-burn mainly due to deficiency of digestive fire and enzymes of body. One should take rock salt with 20 gm ginger after meals. Narayana churan each 2 gm with sugar must be given at bed time. Hing vashtaka churan is another remedy for dyspepsia.

Diarrhoea

Diarrhoea is a condition where stools are passed loosely through the anus. The stools may contain water, formed or semi-formed or solid digested or undigested food in small or large quantity. These may contain virulent bacteria like typhoid, fever, cholera, intestinal tuberculosis, lung infectin, kidney disorders, liver trouble and stomach. Diarrhoea is cuased by the vitiation of vata, pitta and kapha. It sometimes caused due to sudden fright, shock, worry, change of climate or change of diet. To cure diarrhoea, ban all foods except liquids because lack of water may lead to dehydration. Collect the ingredients such as 1 litre freshly boiled mineral water, 2 tbs. of honey, ¼ tsp. of sea salt, ¼ tsp of bicarbonate of soda and a little fresh lemon juice. An adult should take little quantity of this liquid every five minutes and consume atleast three litre within 24 hours. The children need to drink atleast one litre in 24 hours. Another most reliable liquid is to drink Barley water preferably with lemon. Rice water, too, relieves diarrhoea.

Boil 25 gms of rice gently in 1 litre water for 60 to 90 minutes. Strain and drink the liquid to soothe the irritated bowel. A good food for a child who is suffering from diarrhoea is plain boiled white rice mashed up with bananas. Plain live yoghurt kills off unwanted bacteria. The juice of fresh potatoes mixedwith carrot juice and honey clears the bowel of infection. Potatoes which have been cooked and left for over 24 hours before eating are unfit to eat. If an allergic reaction to a food or drug is the cause of sickness and diarrhoea drink two glasses of grape juice and water.

Dysentery

In Ayurveda, it is known as Raktatisara. Dysentery is a condition wherein the patients notice passing of blood in stool alongwith mucus or with faeces or without faeces. It is due to the inflammation of the lower part of the large intestine. The pateient experience pain in the abdomen. The Bael fruit is most beneficial in the treatment of dysentry. The pulp of the fruit mixed with gur may be taken a few times in a day. If there is heaviness in the stomach and the intestines castor oil should be administered with milk to help to eject hard lumps of stools. 2 tsp. of Isphagula (Fleaseed) mixed with about 100 gms of curd should be taken three to four times in the day. Alternatively, 50 gm of seeds of Tulsi should be boiled in ½ litre of water till half of the water is left, the infusion cooled and taken thrice daily. The inner bark of the mango tree is another good remedy. The bark should be steeped in water overnight; it should be expressed in the morning and the water drunk during the day in small doses.

Sprue Syndrome

Sprue or Psilosis also called Sangrahini is characterized by diarrhoea with passage of large fatty stools. The symptoms include a sore tongue, anaemia and loss of weight. An inborn error of the metabolism is the main cause of the disease when the body is denied nutrition, leading to weakness. The condition tends to become chronic if not dealt in the early stages. Emotional stresses and irregularity in meals is a contributing cause.

Important remedy is to grind together in powder equal weights of kernel of old+mango and kernel of Jamun fruits, taken thrice daily with butter milk. Pulp of Bael fruit taken few times in a day is another remedy.

Few digestive disorders

Cholera is a condition characterized by vomiting, diarrhoea and severe pain in the abdomen. The disease is spread through flies, fomites, faeces water and vegetables. In Ayurveda, this disease is called Vishoochika. It can be prevented by the administration of liquid extract of Ajwain (Ark) mixed with coriander water in small doses. Cholera can also be successfully treated by adminstering the juice of onion and bitter gourd. **Thirst** is a desire for water which occurs whenever there is a great demand for water in the body - in which the patient has dryness in the throat. The patient is given butter milk with a little quantity of sugar, honey and ghee. **Colic pain** is produced due to the causes which may produce indigestion and stomach disorders. It is called amayshaya shoola in Ayurveda. Ginger juice mixed with castor oil will relieve the pain.

What is tonic?

A tonic is something that invigorates, restores, stimulates or refreshes. The usual contents of the currently popular tonics are vitamins and minerals. Vitamins are naturally occuring biochemical either by the body or made available from food stuffs like meat, fish, eggs, vegetables and fruits. An average diet contains a sufficient amount of vitamins. The excess and shortage of vitamins, both are harmful and produce adverse effects as shown below.

Composition of Vitamins and their effect

Vitamin-A (Daily requirement 3000-4000 I.U). Available in Ghee, Butter, Egg, Fish, Green vegetables (Carrots & Spinach). Effect of deficiency include rough and dry skin and diminished vision. Adverse affects are headache, body aches, nausea, vomiting, itching skin and loss of hair.

Vitamin-D (Daily requirement 400 I.U.). Available in Fish, Egg, Butter, Milk and sunglight. Deficiencies include decreased bone growth in children, thinning of bone in adults. Adverse effects are loss of appetite, diarrhoea, kidney failure, deposition of calcium in tissues, nervousness, trembling, headache and muscle weakness.

Vitamin-B Complex or Vitamin B-1 (Daily requirement 1-5 mg). Available in Cereals, pulses, meat, dairy products, vegetables, nuts and fruits. Deficiency include weakness and nervousness. Adverse effects are nervousness, trembling, headache and muscles weakness.

Vitamin B_2 - (Daily requirement 2 mg). Found in most foods. Deficiency include ulcers in mouth, burning sensation in eyes and scaliness of skin.

Nictotine Mide (Daily requirement 20 mg). Available in Liver, meat, fish, cereals and pulses. Deficiency include diarrhoea, mental symptoms, ulcers in mouth, headache, insomnia. Adverse effects are liver damage, peptic ulcer, nausea, vomiting, diarrhoea, increase in blood sugar.

Vitamin-B_6 - (Daily requirement 2 mg). Available in meat, fish, cereals, pulses and yeast. Deficiency include ulcers in mouth, nerve damage and anaemia. Adverse effects are pimples, skin rashes and convulsions.

Folic acid (Daily requirement 0.1 mg). Available in liver, eggs, leafy vegetables. Deficiency include anaemia, soreness of tongue, weakness. Adverse effects are kidney damage and insomnia.

Vitamin B_{12} (Daily requirement 2-3 mg). Available in Liver, fish, egg and milk. Deficiency include anaemia, sterility and nerves damage.

Vitamin C (Daily requirement 50 mg). Available in Citrus foods green vegetables and pulses. Deficiency include weakness, anaemia and swelling of gums. Adverse effects are diarrhoea, kidney stone and effect on unborn baby in womb among pregnants.

Alcohol

Alcohol is a food which provides energy quickly than any other food. It is rich in calories and carries 7 calories per gram while carbohydrates provide 4 calories and fats provide 9 calories per gram. A bottle of beer (650 ml) contains 250 calories, 100 ml of whisky carries 400 calories. Alcohol go into the blood stream in the body. After reaching the blood, it goes to other parts of the body, but in liver, it is primarily metabolizes to carbon-dioxide and water. Many peple are of the impression that alcohol is a sex stimulant, but it is not necessarily mean. However, alcohol removes shyness and promotes sexual advances, but the sex act, if it takes place, suffers. Alcohol should never be taken on a empty stomach. Avoid taking alcohol if you suffer from a liver or kidney disease or peptic ulcer. Alcohol has several useful applications. As a skin antiseptic 70% alcohol is very useful. Three parts of rectified spirit should be diluted with one part of water to make it 70% before application. Alcohol in a concentration of 50%, if rubbed, prevents development of bed sores.

4

Ayurvedic Treatment for Acne and Scars

Acne is caused by an increase in androgen hormone activity, which stimulates the functioning of the sebaceous glands. The shedding of the dead skin cells cause blockage within the hair follicle, which become infected. An overgrowth of the skin over the pores is another prominent factor. The skin's normal covering of the bacterium becomes more active, and multiply rapidly. Anti-bacterial products cause inflammation not only in the hair follicle but also on the surrounding area. Acne usually starts to develop around adolescence in both male and female which clears up after 5 to 10 years. In some older people acne can sometimes develop spontaneously. The face is the usual site of acne, although it can also appear on the chest, neck,

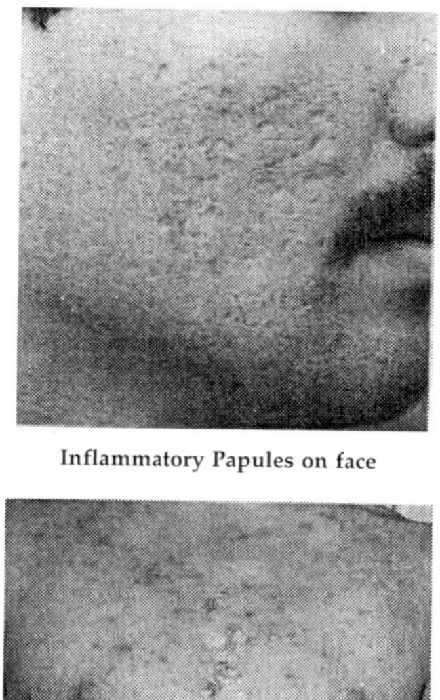

Inflammatory Papules on face

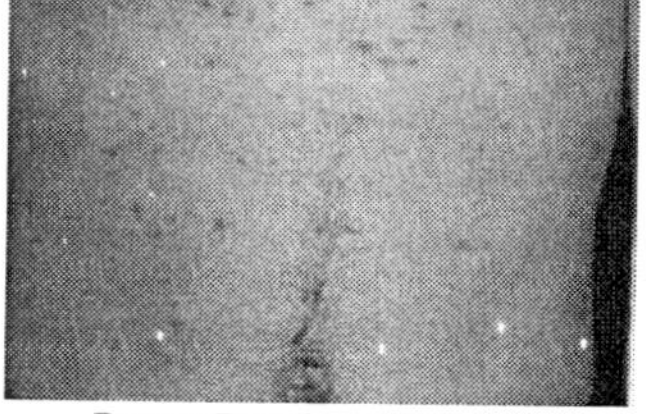

Poputo-Pustules after Acne

shoulders, back, scalp, legs and upper arms. Acne usually consists of **Blackheads** (blocked matter in the pores oxygenate and turns black), **Comedones** (pores becoming blocked with a mixture of sebum and dead skin cells), **Nodules** (inflamed area causing scarring), **Papules** (inflamed area without infection), **Pustules** (inflammation, containing pus), **Scarring / macules** (if the skin is treated incorrectly), **White-heads** (when the pores has closed, trapping matter inside). The hormonal imbalance, allergic reduction, poor diet are the major cause for the adrenal glands to be stimulated, leading to hormonal imbalances, which mostly occur during adolescence and occasionally during the menopause in women and also prior to periods may all create the conditions under which acne erupt.

Acne treatment - the herbal ways

Cleansing should consist of the product containing an anti-inflammatory substance being smoothed over the face with a disposable fabric or cotton wool. Wipe the cleanser off carefully with appropriate hydrolat such as thyme, myrtle, lemongrass, lavender or camomile german with disposable fabric or cotton wool. Repeat cleansing process twice. Apply a compress of green tea (camilla sinensis) on the face and leave for five minutes. Dry the face. Apply blend of essential oil in the appropriate base oil. Gently press oil on the face, starting at the chin and working up the face in sections towards

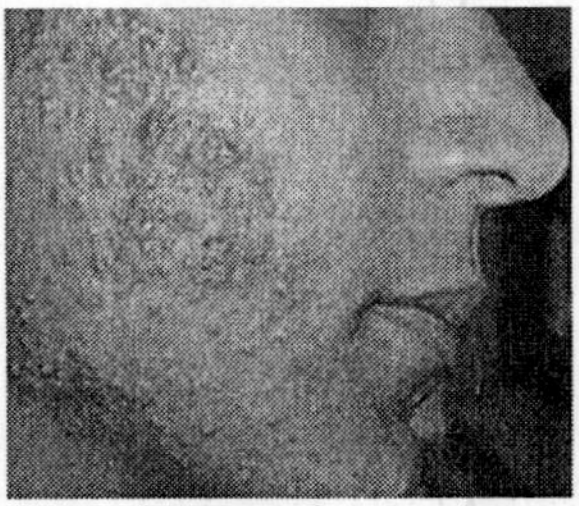

Pitted Scars due to Acne

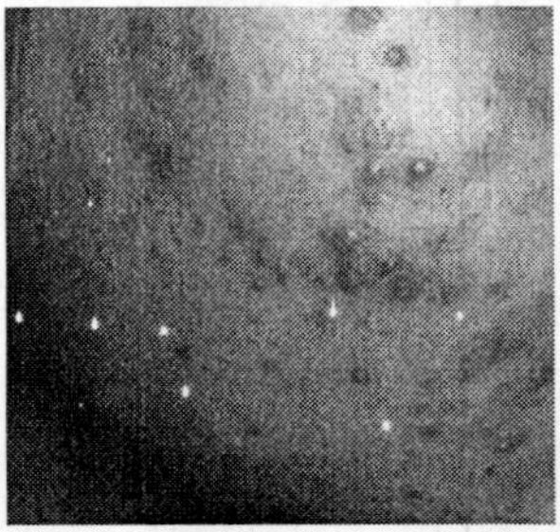

Cystic Lesions on Body

the forehead. Apply a warm, damp, green tea muslin compress over the top of the oil. If there is no acne on the neck, gently place your hands on the trapezius muscle and in continuous flowing movement use long strokes, moving towards the occipital. Start with the right hand followed by the left hand. Repeat six times. Do not massage the face itself rapidly, this may cause further inflammation. Start at the middle of the sternum, (Bone running from neck to stomach). Use effleurage in a smooth movement towards the armpits. Gradually work in sections outwards until the clavicle (collar bone) is reached. Use small circular movements with the middle finger, following the bone outwards towards the armpits. Repeat the above movements on the upper side of the clavicle, following the bone. Then wipe your hands thoroughly.

Now treat reflex points. Start at the forehead. Harmonise energy by holding the face in both hands for few seconds. If using a compress, leave for one to three minutes. If using a poultice, leave for five minutes. Now apply mask, leave it on the face for not more than ten minutes. Finish by wiping with a hydrolate. Place both hands on shoulders in the energy harmony position. Relax for few minutes, then have a glass of water to drink. To complete treatment, rub hands briskly but gently up the vertebrae. Leave skin free for atleast 24 hours.

Ayurvedic steps to get rid of pimples and acne

Pimples can mar many a lovely skin, besides scarring it permanently. Pimples generally crop up on the cheeks, forehead and nose. The following ayurvedic home remedies can work wonders:

- Make a paste of the barks of neem and turmeric (haldi)

and rub on the affected area. Another remedy is to rub a piece of sandalwood on a clean stone using rose water or cucumber juice to make a paste. This pack gives a tingling fresh feeling and will discourage pimples. Multani mitti pack is an effective means to control pimples. Dissolve Fuller's earth (multani mitti) in water to make a thin paste. Smear over the affected skin, and wash with cold water when it dries.

- Mix one part of slake time with 20 parts water. Mix it to two parts finely powdered sulphur. The mixture should be boiled till half the quantity is left. Apply a light coat of fluid to the pimples and acne. Take a spoonful of honey mixed with water and lemon juice in the morning daily. Crush mint to make a paste and apply the pack thrice a week. Wash the face with cold water after ten minutes. Mix gram-flour in a spoonful of coconut oil and rub it on the affected skin. When it dries wash the face with mild hot water. Onion mask is used on blemished oily skin. Mix together 1 tbs. onion juice, 1 tbs. kadin powder and 1 tsp. clear honey. Apply formed thick paste on the skin.
- Use sulphur soap to keep oil glands open. Steam your face once a week to clean skin pores. Do not peel off pimples that cause septic and may leave behind permanent scars. Cleanse stale make-up at night before going to bed. Cut down on sweets, fats and spicy dishes. A sulphur mask helps a lot. Mix together 1 tsp. sulphur powder, 2 tbs fuller to earth, 1 beaten egg white and little rose water to make a smooth paste. This is an effective cleansing mask. Make an allergy test before using it because some skins suffer an adverse reaction to sulphur. Spread a little mixture over the skin on elbow; leave for 10 minutes to check reaction. There are several other factors in treating acne. Sunlight usually discourages pimples and acne. And the tan

disguises some of the redness. Antibiotic lotions containing clindamycin or erythromycin are successful in treating pimples and acne. Consult a doctor before using such lotions as many antibiotics darken the skin.

- Oestrogens hormones have long been used in the treatment of pimples in young women, however, the doses required are high and it is not desirable. In men the doses of oestrogens required to be effective are too high and unacceptable. Peeling agents help by opening up of follicles. Benzoyl peroxide or Ritinoic acid (Vit. A acid) can be used for this purpose. These are available in creams and produce redness and soreness as well as peeling. The frequency of application should be reduced to once or twice a week, as soon as peeling starts. Tetracycline is recommended in low doses of 250 mg (one hour before breakfast for three months or more). These small doses are montoxic and involves reduction in the formation of irritant fatty acids in pimples. Except for local injection into the pimple, corticosteroids should not be used. It suppress pimples for a few days but after that they reappear with venegeance. Prolonged use of corticosteroids for pimples sometimes lead to serious adverse affects, so have treatment in consultation with a doctor.
- Pimple-like eruptions on the face often seen in young persons between the age of 16 to 21 (also called puberty boils) can be treated with Homoeopathic medicines Kali Brom (used in 6 to 30 potency), Asterias Rubens (in case of red pimples on the side of nose, chin and mouth), Radium Bromide (in 30 potency), Berberis Aqua Follum (effective in case of girls), Dulcamara (in case pimples appear before menses) and Ars 1000 and Sulphur, Iodide 3×Trit (when the number of pimples is too excessive).
- Skin with acne needs to be treated very gently, particularly if the harsh commercial and prescription products have previously been used and have not been

found helpful. The percentage of essential oil used depends on the type and severity of the acne being treated, varying between 2 to 3 percent. The compress plants useful for acne cure/treatments include Calendula, Marigold, Camomile German and Camomile Roman, Lavender, Melissa, Peppermint, Rosemary, Sage, St John's Wort and Yarrow. The essential oils useful for treating acne skins are Bergamot, Cedarwood, Cypress, Euclyptus Radiata, Geranium, Juniper, Lemon, Lemongrass, Neroli, Palmarosa, Patchouli, Peritgrain, Tea Tree, thyme Linalol and Vetiver.

Ayurvedic Face Packs for Acne and Scars

Face packs are used for toning of tired skin. Face pack has property similar to Toner. A pack should always be applied after applying a scrubber which opens the pore due to scrubbing effect. Therefore, it becomes very necessary to close down the pores with the help of face pack. On a wrinkled or excessive dry skin, remove the mask when it semi-dries. After washing the face pack, apply rose water, it prevents the skin from drying. Face packs are of several types. An Anti Sun Tan pack is most suitable for all type of skins; use it with rose water and lemon juice for best result and a uniform complexion. Sandal Face pack is also suitable to tone up all types of skin when used with rose water and glycerine for excellent result. Both packs help to lighten the blemishes. Tulsi Face pack is most suitable for acne or pimply skin. For best result use it with toner or an astringent lotion. Neem Face pack

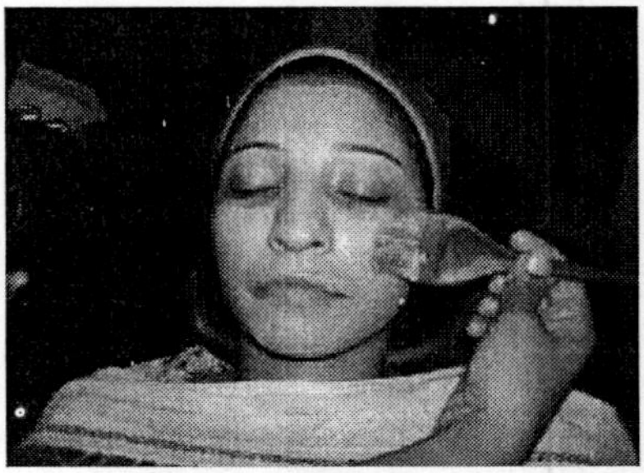

Applying Face Pack

having antiseptic properties suit an acne, pimple and scarred skin. Cucumber Face pack has cleansing and toning properties and suit a dry to normal skin. Use it with rose water for best result. This pack is suitable for dull, tired, tan skin. Egg Face pack tightens a dull, wrinkled skin when used with rose water or a toner. Orange Face pack controls excessive oil from an oily skin when used with a astringent. Mint Face pack and a Thermoherb pack (on the face applied on a gauge) are suitable for normal skin when used with rose water.

Ayurvedic Skin Care Products

A skin toner has the property to tone the skin. It reduces the pore size, prevents excess sweating and sebum secretion. Toner is recommend for normal to dry skin. An aloe vera toner is a soothing and softening agent and removes tanning. Cleansing milk has property to open pores and draw out the dirt, dried sweat and sebum. After cleansing, apply a toner or astringent for reclosing the pores of the skin. Sun Screen Lotion has the property to reflect back light. The pigment called melanin present in the skin, is affected by sun rays which produce and stimulate melanin. Sunscreen forms a layer on the skin and hence prevent the rays from stimulating the production of melanin. Astringent is used by oily skin. Even normal and dry skins can use it but it is more useful for oily skin. Moisturiser is essential for all types of skins. Wheatgerm oil is a rich oil having high content of Vit. E. Olive oil is also rich in Vit. E. Healthy skin needs high proportion of Vit. E in the skin. Rose water has natural property of toning. Cold cream, too, has good moisturising property and prevents dryness. It is easily absorbable because of having waxy base.

Massage cream is usually light weight, non-greasy and easily absorbable cream. Spa Therapy is also used for relaxation of muscle, which leave relaxing effect on the facial muscles and a lot of glow is observed after the massage. An all purpose cream, light in weight and easily absorbable, can be used for any purpose such as massage, to prevent dryness, for softness and glow to the skin. Almond Nourishing Cream is considered as the best remedy for any skin problem. Almond has high content of Vit. E which gives nourishment to the skin. The beginning of any undernourished skin starts from under eye problem. Almond cream revives back the skin texture and brings glow on the skin. Calamine lotion helps remove pimples, acne, scar and also has sun-screening agents in it. It can be used for cosmetic purpose also. Being non-greasy and light; it spreads on face uniformly and evenly giving a natural look to skin. For years Tulsi has been known for its antiseptic and antibacterial properties. Tulsi Pomade protects the skin from becoming dry, it heals dry, chapped and cracked skin. Petroleum Jelly also protects the skin from drying, and nourishes it.

Prevention is better than cure

A person falls sick when his defences are weak. When his vital force is at a low ebb. It is the vital force that keeps you alive and strong against disease and decay. The vital force is the storehouse of your physical strength, your vigour, your ebullience and your verbe. A sickly pale face is due to lack of blood in the body, malfunctioning bowels and diminishing vital force. For that a person has to follow simple and basic rules with regard to sleep, fresh air, sunlight and clean habits - all these play an important role. Mental make-up is closely related to health, stress, anger, frustration, worry, envy, jealously and violent reactions are harmful to human body, mind and soul. Your way of life leaves its imprint on your health. Remember your skin is the mirror for your health. Facial scars, wrinkles, freckles, scabies, eczema, ringworm, boils and pustules mar a lovely skin leaving scars on the face. Skin may not appear to be a vital - an organ as the heart or brain is, but nevertheless presence of intact skin is essential for life, to maintain a good personality, self confidence and self respect in society. The skin disorders fall into four categories: Disorders of the secreting apparatus, Skin affliction relating to unwanted scars (like boils, rashes, spots on the skin); Inflammatory conditions and Nervous & parasitic infections.

The human skin consists of two main layers - the cuticle or epidermis and the true skin or dermis (also known as cutis vera). The true skin is the fibrous layer having thickness varying from 0.55 mm to 3 mm, being thicker in the males than among the females. The skin has two types of glands : Sebaceous glands which secrete a fatty liquid (called sebum) and sweat glands which secrete perspiration. The skin acts as a protective guard and saves the muscles and regulates body temperature. Discoloration of skin is oftenly mistaken for scarring. Initially all scars are red, pink or purple but the colour fades over a year. The blood vessels in a scarred area may be very noticeable but all colour changes can be camouflaged with make-up or special covering creams. Many scars become temporarily lumpy during healing but later flatten. The skin may darken because of pigments in the skin - two main pigments deposited in the skin are iron and melanin. Colour cells (melanocytes) are studded in large numbers throughout the skin, and they produce a brown pigment called melanin - their amounts varies with colour production by sunshine. The colour of the skin also depends on the blood supply to the skin.

A Lesion is a structural change in the tissues caused by injury or disease, which are of two types: Primary and Secondary. Primary lesions are macule (small discoloured spot or patch neither raised nor sunken on the skin), Papule (small elevated pimple without fluid or developing pus sometimes), wheal (itchy, swollen spot due to mosquito or insect bites), Tubercle (soiled lump projective above or under the surface of the skin), Tumour (external swelling varying in the size, shape and colour), Vesicle (small blister with clear fluid in it, beneath the epidermis), Bulla (large blister containing watery fluid) and Pustule (pimply looking elevation with inflamed base containing pus). Secondary lesions develop in the later stage of the disease which include scale (dry or greasy epidermal flakes), Crust or scab (accumulation of sebum and pus with epidermal material), Excoriation (skin abrasion produced by scratching or scraping due to loss of skin), Fissure (crack in the skin penetrating into the dermis), Ulcer (mucous membrane of the body accompanied by pus), Scar (usually forms after healing an injury or skin condition) and Stain (abnormal discoloration of skin). The common skin diseases include an acute (less violent), a chronic (long duration and recurring), an infectious (caused by pathogenic germs), contagioius (communicable by contact), Congenital (present since birth), Seasonal (influenced by the weather), Occupational (afflicted by one's occupation), Parasitic (caused by a vegetable, or animal parasitic), Pathogenic (produced by a bacteria), Systemic (over functioning of internal glands), Veneral (acquired by contact with an infected person usually during sexual intercourse), Epidemic (that attacks simultaneously large number of persons) and an allergy (caused by contact with foods, cosmetics, medicines and tints resulting in itching, redness, swelling, blisters, oozing, pain, heat and scaling).

How to cure scars?

Cosmetic surgery is carried out as a necessity to enhance the look of a person. A cosmetic surgeon cannot tell before hand whether the skin of a particular individual will respond well or not to surgery, in terms of scarring. Surgeons carrying out life-saving procedures are not as concerned about the look of the skin but most of the patients do not want to be left with a permanent reminder of the suffering. The use of essential oils before or after surgery treatments may not eliminate the scar completely, but may lessen it. Using essential oils in treatments pre-operatively can lead to less scarring and bruising, quick recovery, less stress and tension and possibly less risk of infection. Essential oil treatments prepare the client both physically and emotionally for the surgery. For the body, choose essential oils that have a relaxing effect. For the face, choose those that have energising, toning effect.

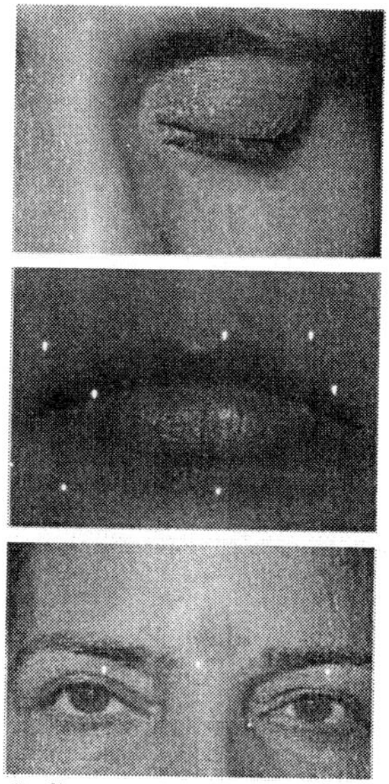

Inflammation on the face

Treatment of new scars

New scars response very well to essential oil blends, which must be applied (not massaged) in the morning and evening for full effect. Choose essential oils that are anti-inflammatory and calming, as these are more effective. Camomile, yarrow, rose and geranium would be good choices. Appropriate carrier or base oils would include camellia oil, macadamia oil, primrose oil, red carrot oil and rosehip seed oil.

Treatment of old scars

Old scars take much longer to respond to treatment. Home care massage will need to be applied every day between treatments. Essential oils that help are frankincense, elemi, rose, geranium, fennel, lemon, orange and carrot seed. Very useful carrier or base oils are rosehip seed oil, borage oil, red carrot root oil and macademia oil. Prepare massage oil for the scar area using the suggested essential oils and vegetable oils. While using less speculised blend on the rest of the body. Herbal ingredients such as camphor, sulphur, onion, garlic, curd, yeast, fuller's earth and vegetable juices are all useful in treating a blemished skin with scars. Here are recipes (mask) which are very beneficial to erade scars. These have healing, soothing astringent and tightening effect on the skin.

Mix together the ingredients such as ½ tsp. Oatmeal, ½ tsp. Camphor BP crystal and 2 tsp. Orange flower water. Apply the mask on the face and leave for 15 to 20 minutes, then wash off with lukewarm water. Two drops of camphor spirit when added to a mixture of one tablespoon tomato juice and one tsp. honey make a strong astringent skin tonic. This tonic should be left on the skin for about 15 minutes to relieve scars. To improve your skin and cure spots apply home-made skin tonic. Mix 1 tbs. glycerine, ½ tbs borax powder to the distilled water and apply on the face.

5

Ayurvedic Tips for Blemished, Spotty Skin

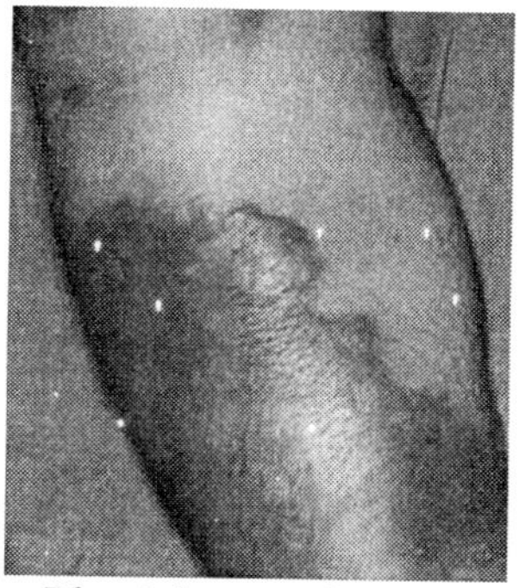

Blemishes on the skin

Rosemary flowers boiled in white wine lighten a sallow skin. A face wash with neat gin softens the wrinkles. Apricot oil rubbed into the most sensitive, soft skin every night before sleep also help. An oily skin may benefit from a covering of mashed strawberries. Hard, leathery patches of skin can be softened with pineapple juice or a mash of papaya as both fruits contain enzymes. A tea made from fenugreek seeds purifies the blood. To clear minor blemishes, apply raspberry mask. Mix 25 gm of mashed raspberries to a paste with 1 tsp. each of plain yoghurt and finely ground oatmeal. Leave on the face for 10 minutes, then rinse

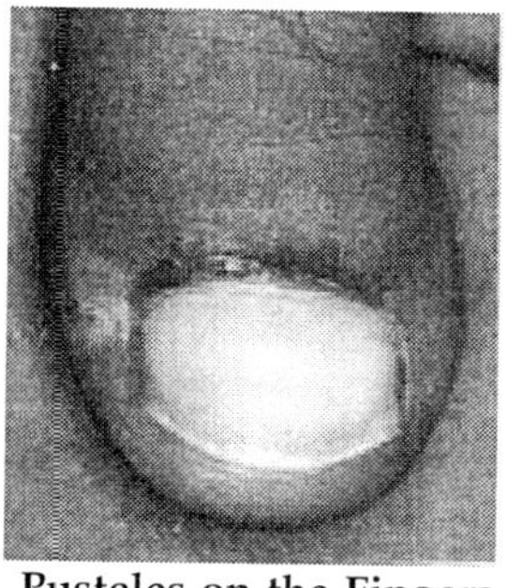

Pusteles on the Fingers

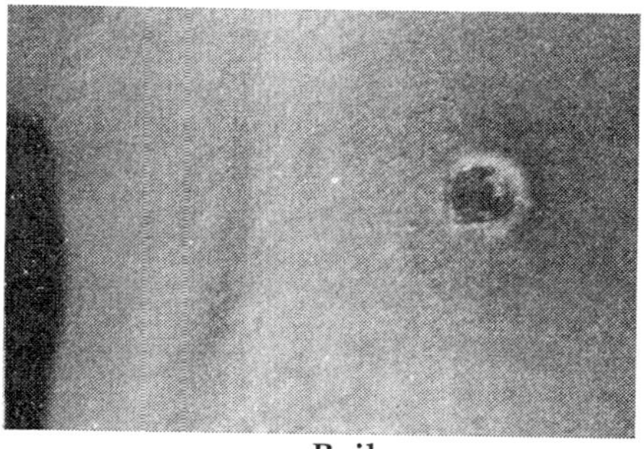

Boil

off. Rubbing raw garlic on a spotty, blemished skin have a fine effect to kill spots. Comfrey, honey and garlic packs help to remedy for persistent pustules. Ground a handful of fresh comfrey leaves with enough honey to make a paste. For each tablespoon take one well mashed garlic clove, apply on a piece of warmed cabbage leaf and tie on affected place on the skin and go to bed. To clear blemishes and spots, here is another night time ointment. Melt 25 gm of beeswax in a bowl on low heat. Add to it 100 gms of pure honey, stir until cool, then pot. Keep in a cool place and apply to infected spots and keep covered the area. Here is another recipe for this. Collect ingredients such as 1 tbs wheatgerm, 2 tsp clear honey, 1 tsp sunflower oil and 1 tsp fresh lemon juice. Mix all the ingredients together to make a thick paste. Apply it in small circular rubbing movements to the face and neck. Leave for five minutes then wash off with warm water. Splash with cold water before patting dry. Use this pack once or twice a week, but avoid soap in between times. Wash your face in clear water only.

AYURVEDIC REMEDIES FOR COMMON DISEASES OF SKIN

Eczema (Dermatitis)

It is a skin condition called 'Pama' in Ayurveda. It is an inflammatory skin disorder in which the cuticle is scaly and fissured with a sticky, watery discharge accompanied by itching and pain over the part. Eczema may be dry or weeping, in which case it ooze. To cure it mix babchi powder with mustard oil and apply like an ointment. Alternatively, the leaves of

Dermatitis

the Indian Butter tree (mahua) should be smeared with sesame oil, warmed over a fire and bandaged on the affected parts. They should be changed after three or four hours. Blood purifying drugs and foods must be administered in consultation with a naturopath. The patient must be advised strict hygiene by taking bath, wearing clean, dried and ironed clothes to prevent further infections. Do not use the towels, utensils and clothes of the infected persons. The patient should not take fresh rice, curd, fish, salt, sour things, milk, jaggery and raddish. Do not indulge in excessive coitus, sleeping during the day and eating too much.

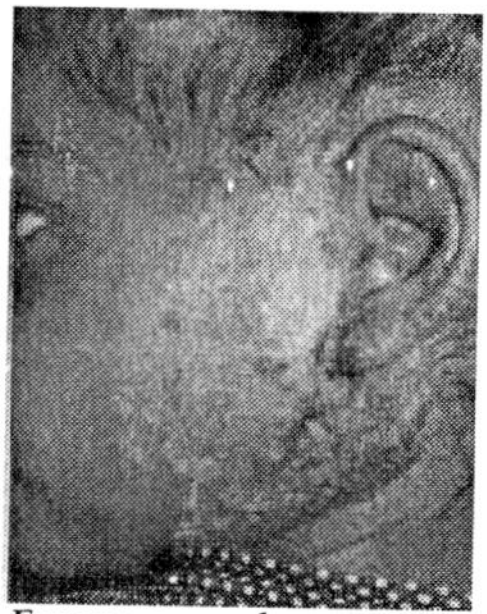

Eczema around ears on face

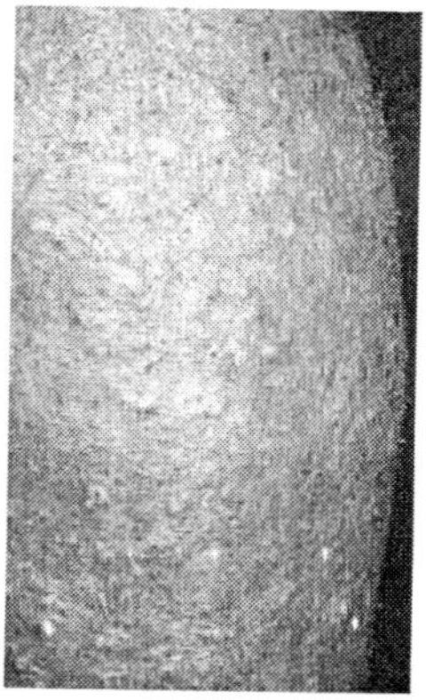

Eczema on back

Scabies (Sarcopties Scabiei)

It is a contagious disease caused by a mite, which lays eggs in burrows in the skin. The disease spreads through contact with infected individual, clothing, bedding or furniture. The commonly affected parts are finger webs, palm, wrist, front of arm, buttocks, soles, area around the nipples, female genitals and penis (among men). The sole complaint is severe itching (excess irritation at night). Sometimes a thin, slimy fluid oozes out of the scratched surface and later forms into scabs. To treat this disorder boil leaves of oleander

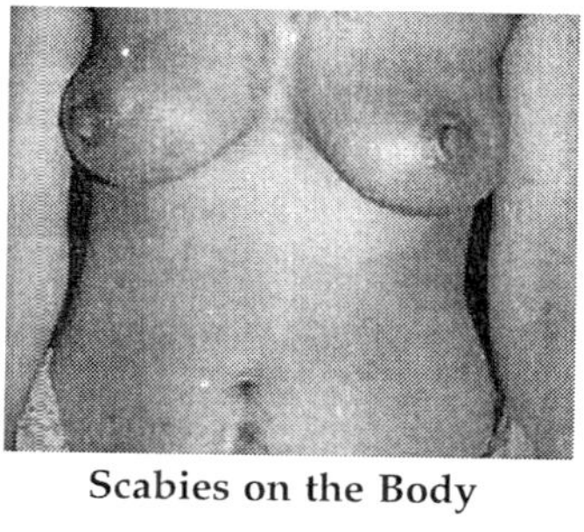

Scabies on the Body

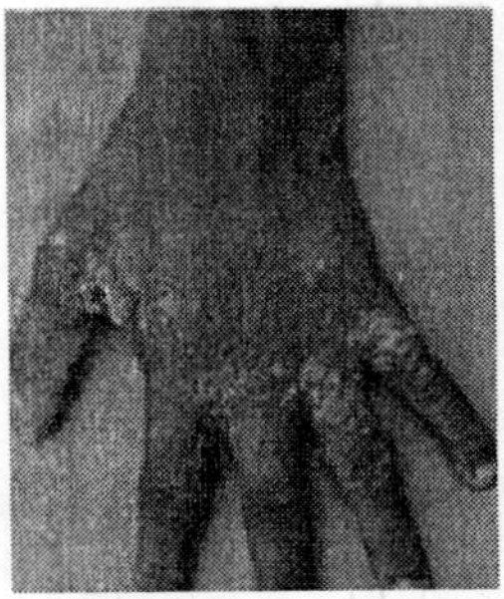

Scabies on Hand

(KARBIR) till charred in 250 ml of mustard oil. The oil should be used for massaging the affected parts. The juice of lemon and jasmine should be mixed and rubbed on the itching surface. Another remedy is ground in water poppy seed. Add to it lemon juice. Massage of this paste relieves dry itch. Gamma benzene hexachloride, used as 1% lotion or cream appears to be a drug of choice in scabies.

Freckles

Ichthyosis Vulgaris

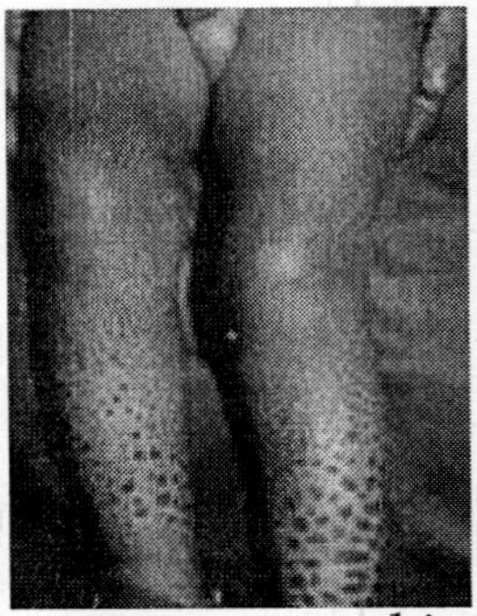

These are brownish spots on the skin due to precipitation of pigments or exposure to the sun. They are caused by a melanin pigmentation in the skin and cannot be removed, only temporarily lightened. Herbal lotions made with elder flower, lime flowers, lemon juice or castor oil are all pressed into use as skin lighteners. To cure freckles ground to a paste pumpkin seeds with olive oil and use to keep skin soft and reduce freckles. The flesh of the pumpkin will also heal red patches and small burns. Another remedy to treat freckles is to ground yellow mustard in the milk and applied to the face at night which should be thoroughly washed in the morning. Alternatively Turmeric and sesame seeds taken in equal quantities and should be grounded in water and applied to the face. Another

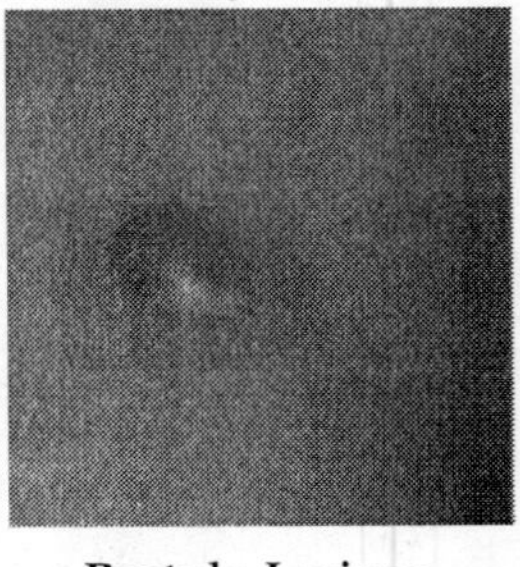

Pustule Lesions

wonderful remedy is to grind the leaves of tulsi in water and apply the paste to the face. An effective drug in the treatment of scabies is Benzylbenzoate, taken in consultation with a doctor. To enable this drug to be effective, it is necessary that the emulsion should be painted by a brush or applied by hand on all over the body except face, neck and head. The drug should be applied on the dried skin after taking a bath and left on for 24 hours, followed by another application. The emulsion should be washed off at the end of 48 hours to enable all mites are killed.

Urticaria (Nettle Rash)

Scaly Lesions due to urticaria

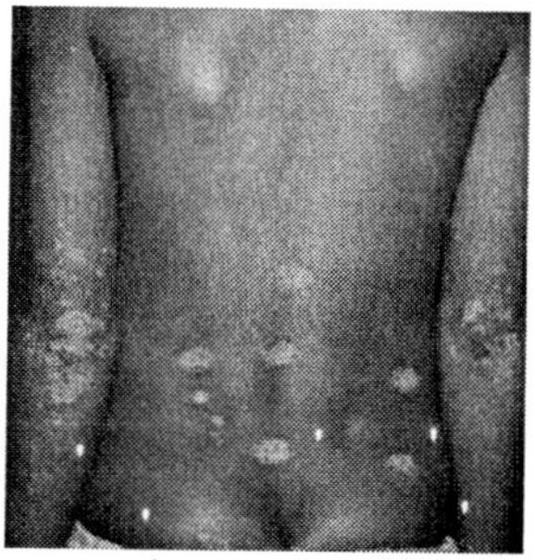

In Ayurveda they are termed as Sheeta Pitta. A disorder of the skin in which weals, rash (raised red and pale Edematous lesions) or pink or white itchy and painful patches appear. Urticarea is caused by allergic conditions of the skin, physical factors like cold, heat, exertion, ultraviolet radiation and psychological stress resulting from sex problems and other problems regarding family employment and finance. Seck medical assistance. Urticaria can be caused by Ayurveda.

Ayurvedic Treatment of Urticaria

The hormonal imbalance, allergic reeaction, poor diet are the major cause for the adrenal glands to be stimulated, leading to hormonal imbalances, which mostly occur during adolescence resembling the sting of a nettle. The main causes to produce this disease are exposure to cold air, taking baths in cold water, psychic situation and intestinal worms. This is nothing but an allergic reaction occurring on the skin. In severe case, there may be an feverishness and constitutional disturbances, together with faintness. To treat uriticaria, mix three parts rose water with two parts of vinegar and the mixture is applied locally to get immediate relief. Another remedy is to mix equal quantity of Alum and Red ochre (Geru) ground together and the powder should be rubbed on the weals. Another Ayurvedic remedy to prevent attacks of urticaria is to grind 1 tsp. Jalneem (Lycopus Europaeus) to 3 tsp Beeswax and the mixture should be made into pills, which should be taken with lukewarm water. Increase the quantity of turmeric in the food. Avoid sour substances. Avoid non-vegetarian meals (especially fish).

Psoriasis

In Ayurveda, it is known as Ekakushta. Psoriasis is a skin disorder identified by silvery-grey, dry, scaly papules on the skin generally on the soft inner side of elbows, knees, and occasionally scalp and forehead. They become rough and red with a silvery soft, scabby appearance. Fair-skinned people suffer from it more oftenly as compared to dark skinned. Psoriasis may be caused by use of detergents or as a result of an allergic reaction. A diet of raw foods including whey milk before breakfast, elm and honey at night is recommended to psoriasis patients besides a diet that

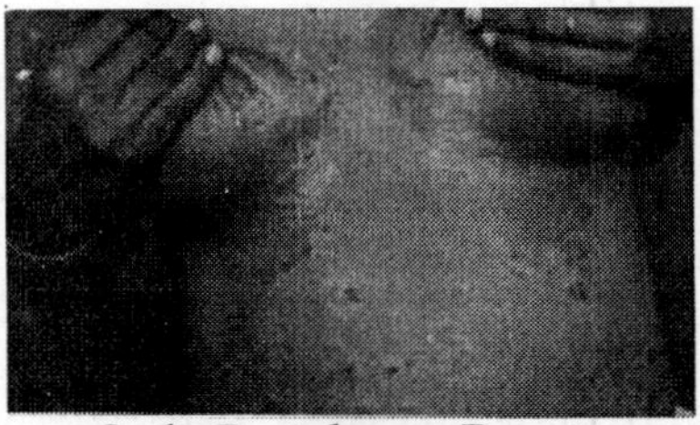

Scaly Pustules on Breast

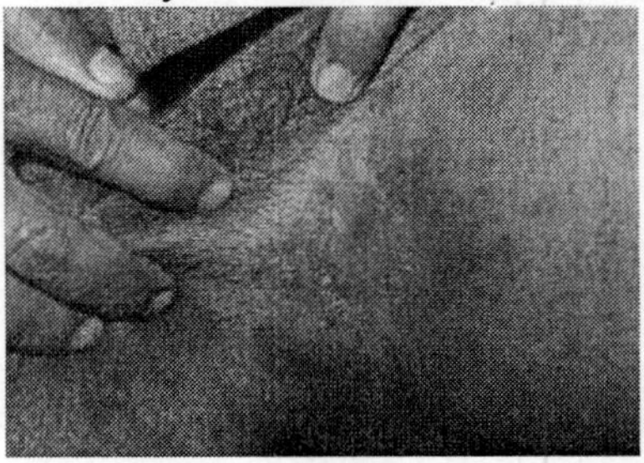

Scaly Pustules on Groin

include Vitamin A suppiement and cold liver oil. Application of witch hazel, nettle extract or calendula (marigold) extract on the affected area of skin with a clean cotton wool soaked in solution relieves irritations. In case of an irritated scalp, boil 4 marigold heads in 4 cups of water for two minutes. Allow to cool, then massage the lotion well into the scalp, wash with a very mild shampoo or a solution of soapwort. Add lemon juice or cider vinegar to the rinsing water to ensure a thorough rinse.

Fungal Infections

Common fungal infections include ringworm, moniliasis and candidiasis. The contagious nature infection Ringworm is called Dadru in Ayurveda in which the patients notice circular scaly patches with severe itching on affected skin or scalp. Rubbing oil of lemon grass mixed with coconut oil or till oil produce highly curative effect. Ringworm can be easily cured by applying either the juice of Marigold leaves or the paste of ground leaves of Genda or Tulsi. Another remedy for the ringworm is; to scratch the patch, then apply to it paste of Borax ground in lime. If the ringworm becomes chronic, it should be rubbed with a coarse cloth and applied to it sap of swallow wort (Akh). Sometimes, ringworm of the scalp leaves an adverse effect. Hot and pungent food is completely forbidden and a diet consisting of milk

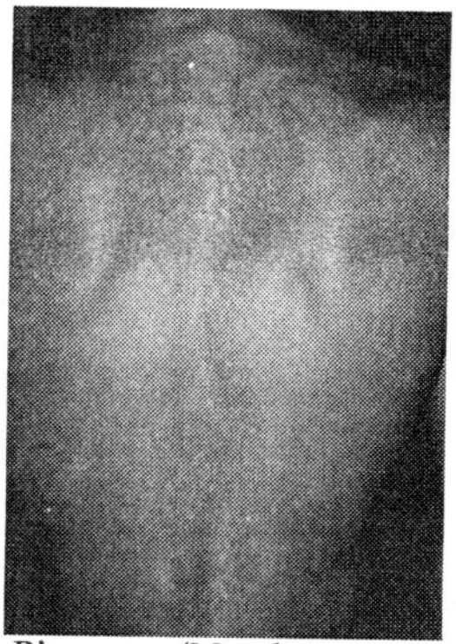

Ringworm (Macule on Back)

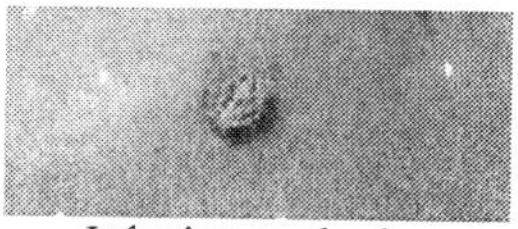

Infection on cheeks

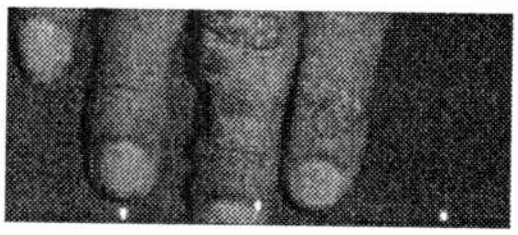

Fungal Infection on fingers

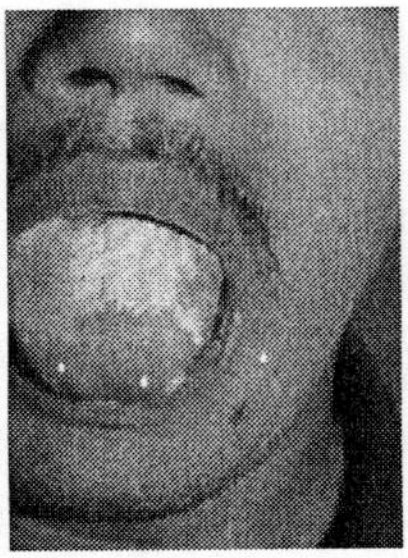

Throsh on Tongue

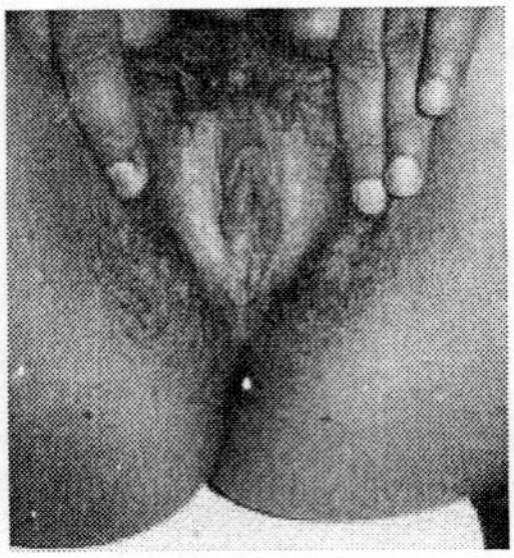

Vaginal Thrush

and rice is strictly advised.

Candidiasis is another form of fungal infection caused by candida albicans. Patients suffering from diabetes mellitus and hypothyroi-dism are usually prone to this infection. It may be associated with the use of oral contraceptives involving skin, intestines and vagina. Doctor usually prescribe an antifungal drug with antibiotics. Always take drug with a fatty meal to allow maximum absorption.

Leucoderma

It is also known as whites - white patches appearing on the skin due to lack of melanin pigment in the skin. Darker skins have more patches because such skins contain more melanin. In Ayurveda it is called Switra or Kilasa. A leucoderma patient is more embarrassed than the victim of any pain or discomfort. In addition to being a medical problem, it also becomes a social stigma. Persons suffering from chronic dysentery and other digestive disorders are more prone to leucoderma than others. Many wrong beliefs are prevalent about the causative factors of leucoderma. The seeds of Babchi are particularly useful in cases of leucoderma. The seeds should be steeped in juice of ginger or a cow's urine for few days. Another useful application is the juice of the leaves of Goose Foot (Bathua); applied to the white spots three to four times a day. The patient should be kept on a salt free and pungent free diet. Exposure to heat should be avoided. A 'chandan' pack is very useful in treating leucoderma. It must be clarified here that white patches are not congenital nor hereditary children are not affected if the mother has these patches. It is also erroneous to think that a woman who has leucoderma does not enjoy marital pleasures.

Leprosy

It affects not only the skin, but also the mucous membranes and the nerves. Leprosy is of two types : tuberculoid and lepromatous. Tuberculoid leprosy is not serious because it run a benign course and is self healing. The Lepromatous leprosy is an infectious disease, in many cases hereditary. It cannot be cured with home remedies. The body of the patient should be massaged with the sap of Neem tree. If the sap is not readily available, five grains of pepper mixed to neem leaves should be ground in water and drunk. Massage with sesame oil or neem oil helps to some extent. The body of the patient should be bathed with water in which leaves of neem and amaltas have been boiled. Have diet in which salt should be as little as possible. Avoid constipation and indigestion, as they aggravate the condition.

Leprosy Ulcer on feet

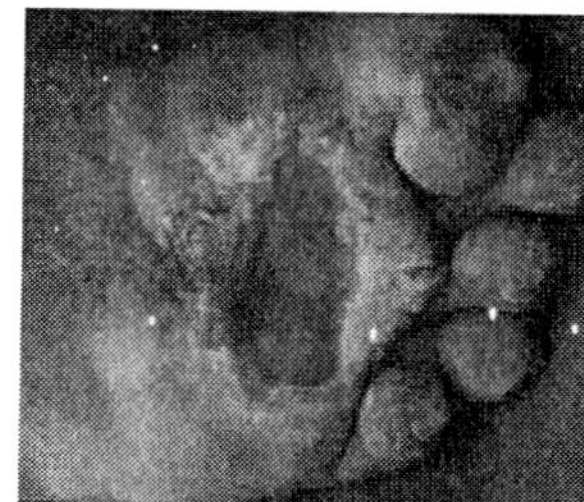

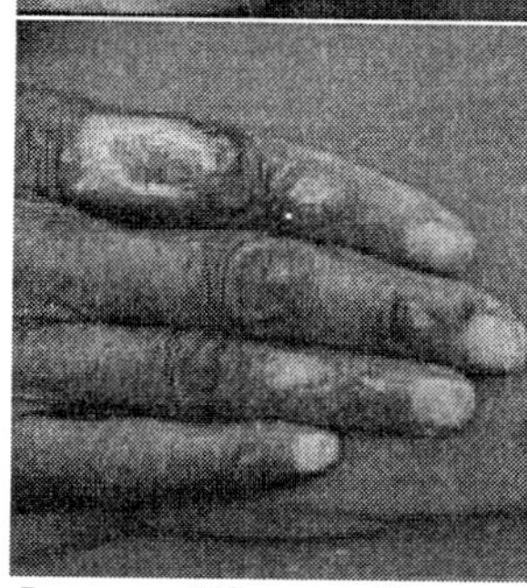

Leprosy Ulcer on fingers

Skin Blemishes

Any kind of spot or number of spots on the face spoil the personality of a woman. The spots and skin disorders are of various kinds. In case of any skin infection or suffering from contagious skin disorder, the matter should immediately be referred to a skin dermatoligist. There are man yAyurvedica recipes to cure various skin disorders.

Erysipelas

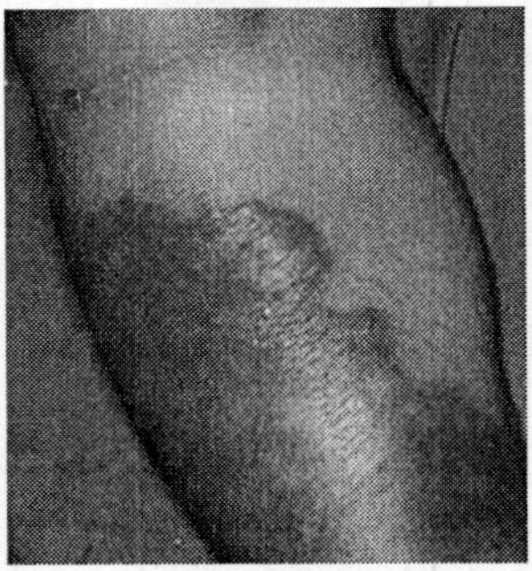

Skin blemishes are temporary problems which may be caused from contact with a rough and bristly surface or to an excess exposure to cold wind. Yoghurt will help to soothe sore patches. Marigold and wheatgerm oil are also helpful to skin disorders. To get rid of spots on the face, the following home remedies should be tried:

- **Garlick Rub:** Rub spots with raw garlick, this will kill them instantly.
- **Night-time Ointment:** Melt 25 gms of bees-wax on low heat. Mix to it 100 gms honey. Stir until cool, then pot, seal tightly and keep in a cool place. Apply this ointment to affected spots at night, then wash it off the next morning.
- **Honey Paste:** Mix the following ingredients together to make a thick paste and apply in circular rubbing movement on the face and neck. Leave for five minutes, then wash off with warm water:

  2 tbs clear honey

  1 tsp wheat-germ oil

  1 tsp sunflower oil

  1 tsp fresh lemon juice

Boils and Pustules

These are red, small, painful nodules which start oozing pus, later leave a tiny scar. These generally occur in the area covered with coarse hair mostly on the neck,

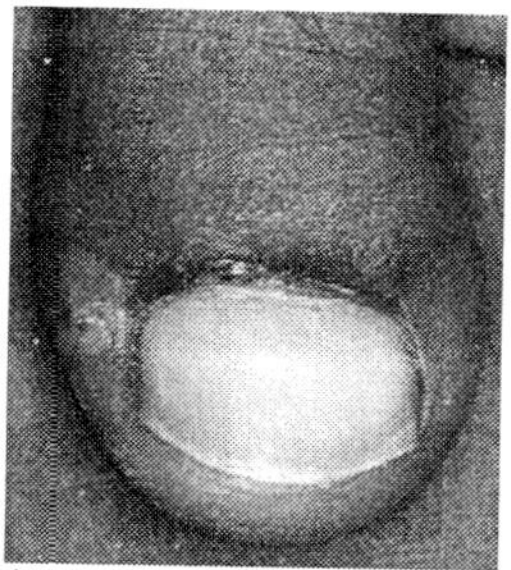

Acute Paronychia (Nail Infection)

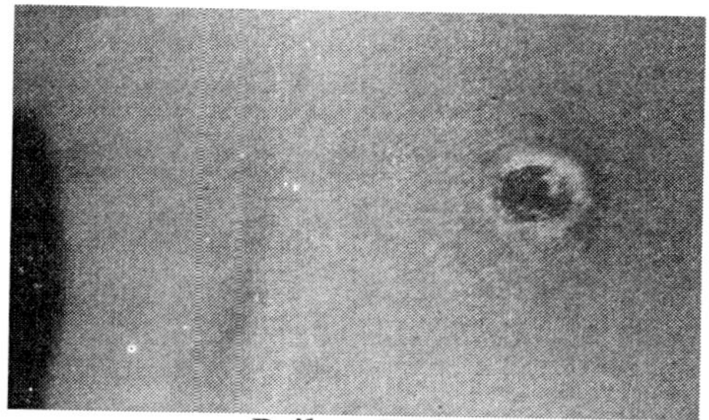

Boil on Back

buttocks, knees and elbows. To treat this skin disorder, take a leaf of 'peepal' tree. Smear it with ghee and apply as lukewarm bandage on the boil. It will burst after sometime. Affected areas include arms, knees, elbows, ankles and knuckles. Depigmentation on forehead is caused by the adhesive of plastic bindi, on breast by the plastic purse generally kept under the bra, on the fold of ear by spectacle frame, on the feet by rubber straps of the slippers and on the waist due to tight pressure caused by the petticoat string.

Hirsutism

These are unwanted coarse hairs in the beard in women.

Unwanted Hairs on Face

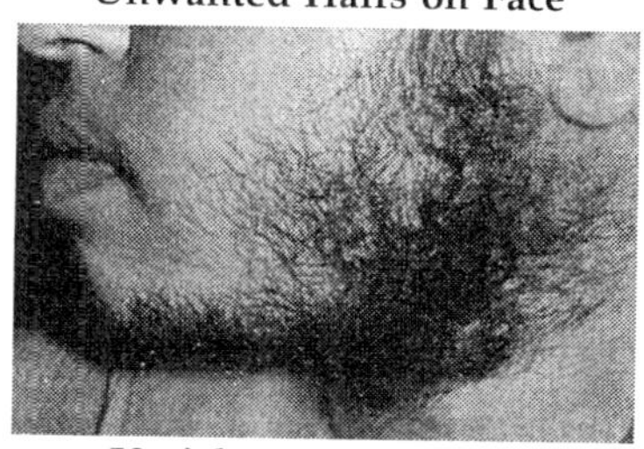

Herpes Simplex

The attack of herpes is usually severe. The lesions generally consists of multiple small vesicles or superficial ulcers on the upper lip of the face (in women), on the glans penis and the shaft of penis (in males). If the attack is mild, the lesions tend to heal in 10 to 14 days. If the infection is severe, an antibiotic treatment recommended by a doctor is essential.

Vesicles on Upper Lips

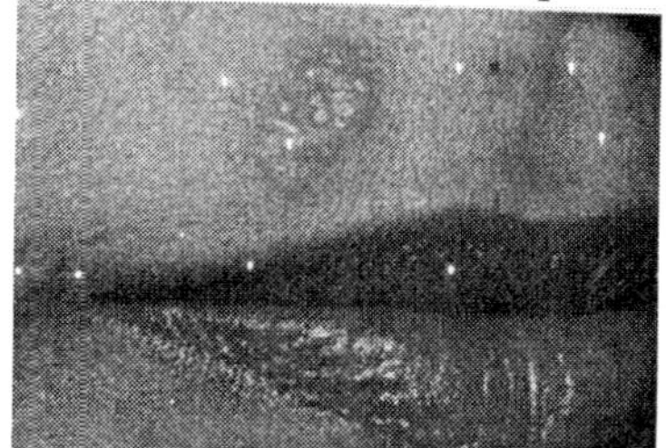

Herpes Zoster

Vesicles on Shaft of Panis

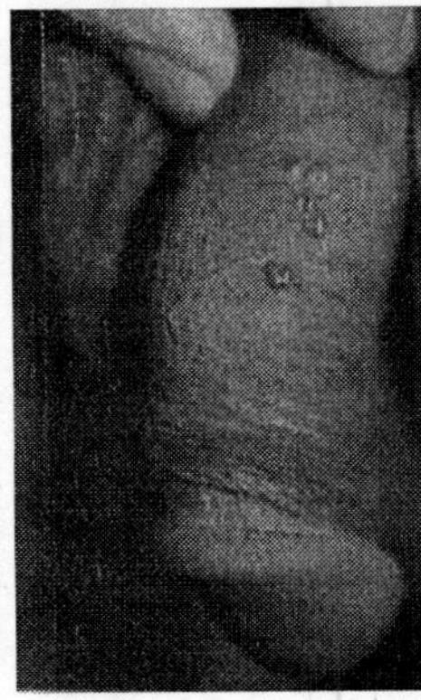

Herpes Zoster— a virus infection is commonly called 'Blisters', which usually appear on genital area, thighs and buttocks. The group of little blisters are painful, tender and highly infectious and burst in the meantime. Herpes Zoster is caused by the same virus as the chicken pox, usually caught by having sex with someone who has Herpes (in case of genital herpes) when group of little blisters appear on the genital area. Remedies to cure Herpes Zoster include:

- Soothing these with essential oils of lemon, geranium, camomile or levender. The essential oils may be diluted in a base oil and rubbed on to the rash.
- Take 25 gms each of dried mullein, mellow roots and marshmallow roots. Put them to simmer for three minutes in three litres of water. Strain and use on a compress throughout the day and night to reduce heat and irritation.

  Common warts are treated by electrocautery in which warts are removed with a cautery which excises the wart with an electric current.

Genital Warts

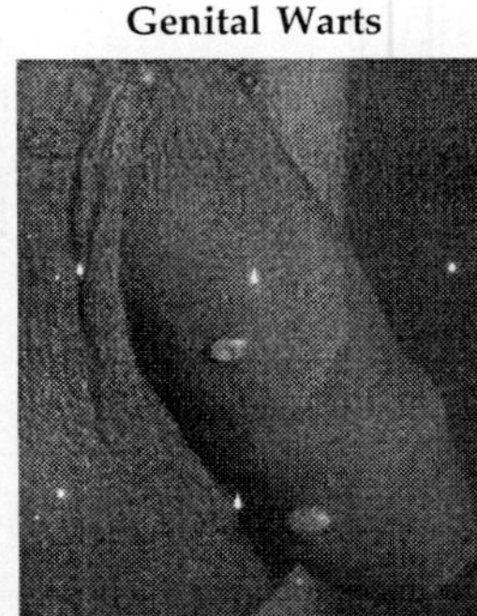

Genital warts (called Candylomata acuminata) produce fungative growth on the glansin men, on valve in women and around the anus. Genital warts are transmitted by contact in the sexually active. They may be related to the development of cervical cancer. So if you have genital warts, get them treated and have cervical smears.

Pickly Heat

Red pustules of size of mustard grains appear on the body, especially on the chest, back and the abdomen. It is caused due to profuse sweating during hot and rainy season. Try the following herbal remedies:

- Apply green heena ground in water on affected skin.
- Grind leaves of neem in water and apply on the affected skin.

Ringworm

Scaly patches on back
(Pityriasis Versicolor)

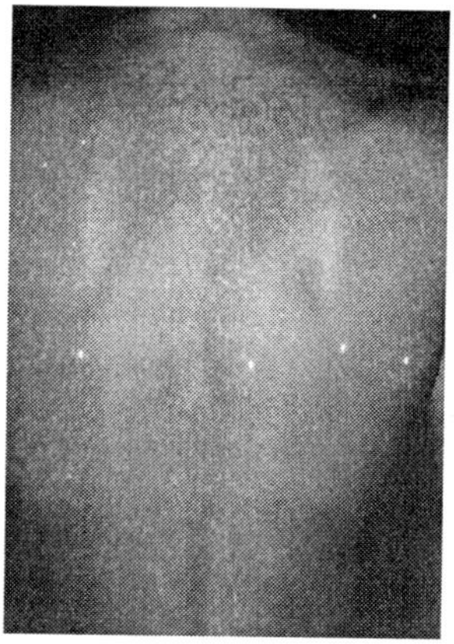

Round patches are formed on the body especially between the legs, on the face, the neck, the back and on the buttocks. This malady is caused due to inflammatory infection of the skin produced by certain moulds, sometimes due to the effect of extreme temperature. As a cure the following remedies are suggested:

- Make a paste of marigold leaves and apply on the affected skin.
- Make a paste of basil leaves and apply on affected skin.
- Scratch the affected skin and apply a paste of borax powder mixed to lime juice.

Allergy

Occasionally, irritation and inflammation of the eyes can be caused by conjunctivitis which may be the result of an allergic reaction. The following remedies are suggested:

- Use olive oil to soothe inflamed eyelids.

- Collect the following ingredients:

  50 gms White wax or Paraffin wax or Bees wax

  300 ml Olive Oil

  100 ml Pure White vinegar

Melt oil and wax together in a bowl held over boiling water. In another bowl gently heat the vinegar in the same way. Remove both bowls from the heat and beat the vineger slowly into the oily mixture until cools.

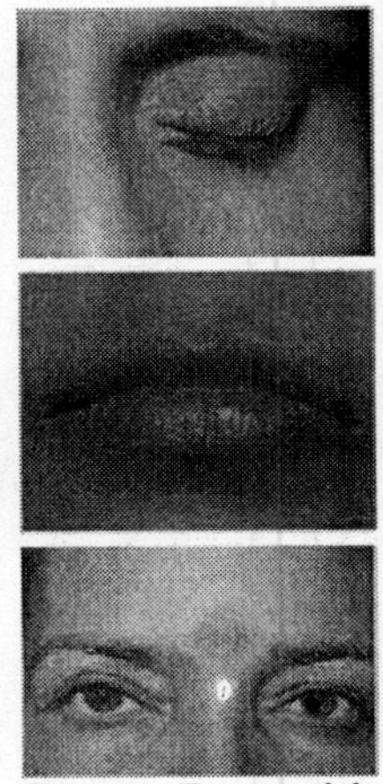

Contact Dermatitis

- Place 50 gms dreed bilerries in a stainless steel pan containting 900 ml of lukewarm water and leave for one hour. Now boil the liquid for 15-20 minutes, remove from the heat and leave until it cools. Strain and use. Drink a small glass or a cup three times daily.
- A poultice made of raw grated carrots is a very old remedy for skin allergy.

Warts

Warts are small epidermic growths caused by a virus. These growths vary in size and shape and are commonly of three types: Plane warts, common warts and planter warts. Plane warts are the simplest of all

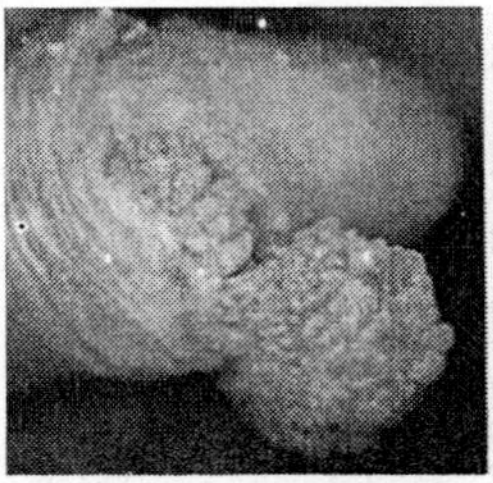

Genital Warts

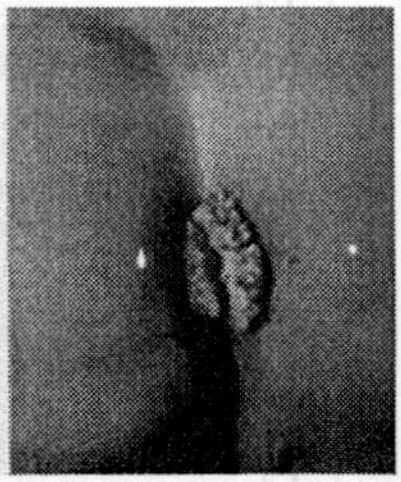

Perinal Warts

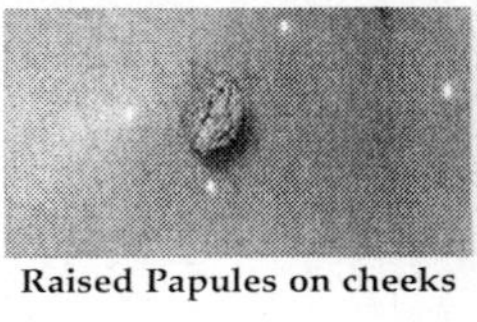

Raised Papules on cheeks

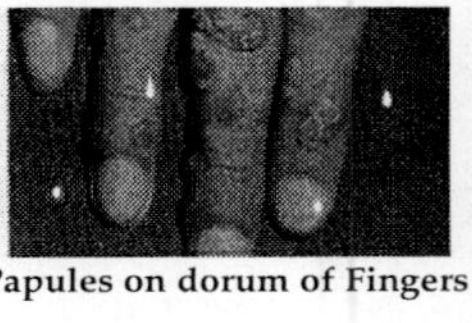

Papules on dorum of Fingers

warts, usually small, smooth and skin-coloured or brownish lesions which are raised slightly from the skin surface. They usually occur in the face and outer surface of the hands. The most commonly affected are children and young adults. Common warts are larger and firmer elevations with a rough surface uaually occur on the hands, forearm, knees and the feet. Planter warts are slighly different. They normally contian blood vessels and bleed because of this. The treatment of warts consists in eleminating them either by chemical lotion or physical means. A peeling agent like 4 percent sulphur calamine lotion or Retino A cream applied daily remove warts. Freezing the wart with liquid nitrogen or carbon snowhelp a lot.

Scabies

An infectious disease usually transmitted from one individual to the other caused by the mite or sometimes from the pet animals e.g. dog, cat, horse and cattle. The itching lesions (more severe at night) are commonly seen on hands, wrists, elbows, axillae, lower part of abdomen, breast folds, thighs, buttocks and penis and scrotum in males. The infection sometimes produce pustules, crusts and lymphadenopathy.

Scabies on Body

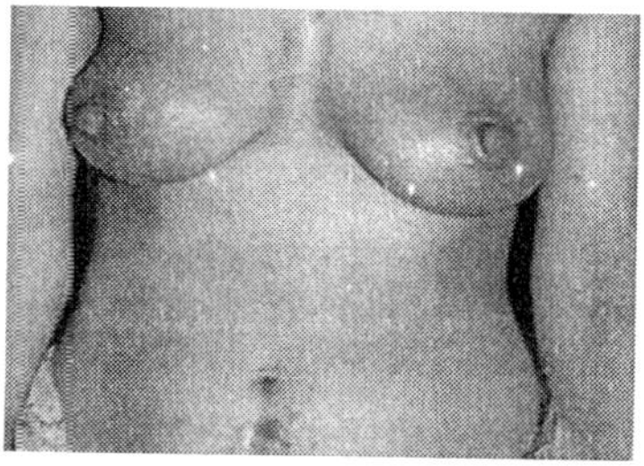

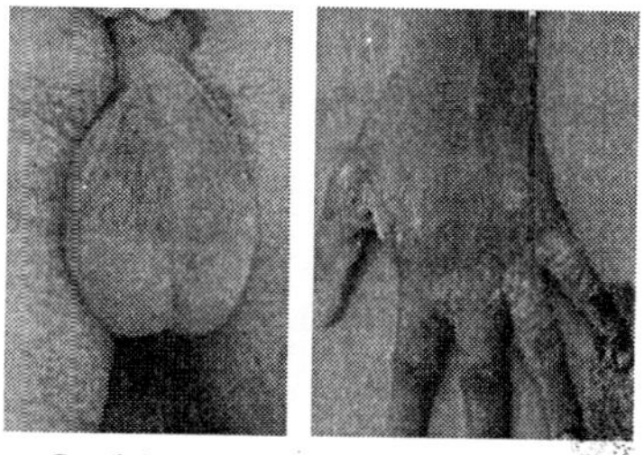

Scabies attack male genitals (Testes) and hands

Angular Stomatitis

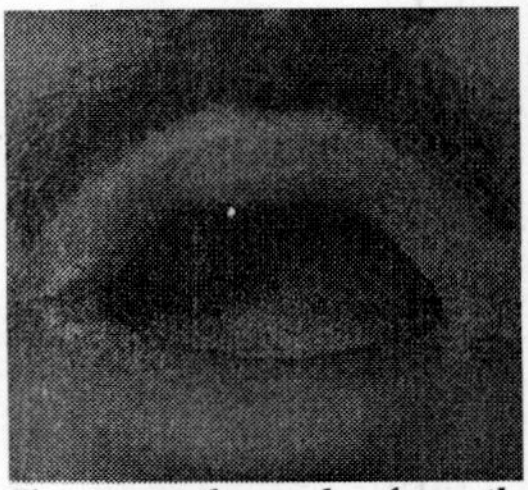

Fissures at the angle of mouth (Angular Stomatitis)

Caused by deficiency of Vitamin B complex group. It manifests as a proliferative growth with a fissure at the angle of mouth.

Cheilitis

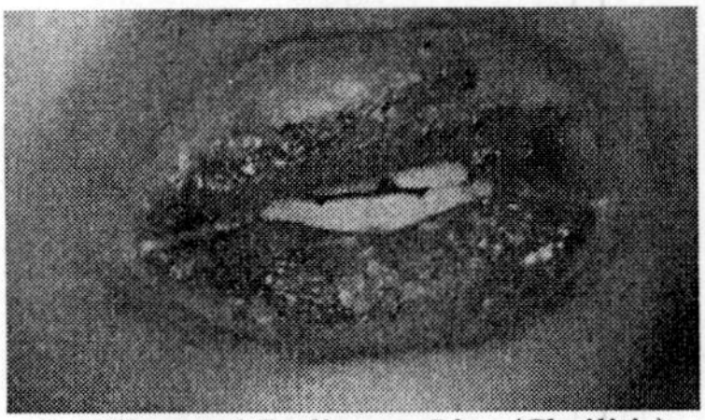

Swelling and Scaling on Lips (Cheilitis)

Usually redness, scaling and swelling appear on both lips.

Chilblains

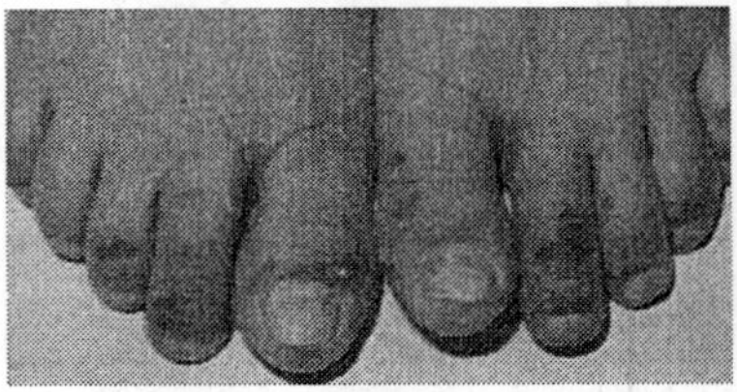

Lesions due to exposure to cold (Chilblains)

These appear on exposure to cold which cause lesions that consist pain, brownish-black discoloration on toes and fingers. Protect from cold and use vasodilators. Antibiotics treatment is recommonded. The area should be scrubbed, dried and smeared with ghee or mustard oil.

Candidiasis

Cured like Whitish deposit on mucosa

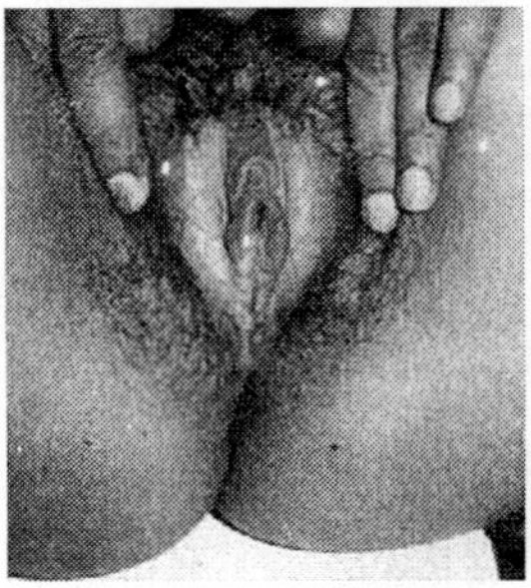

White curd like deposit on toungue

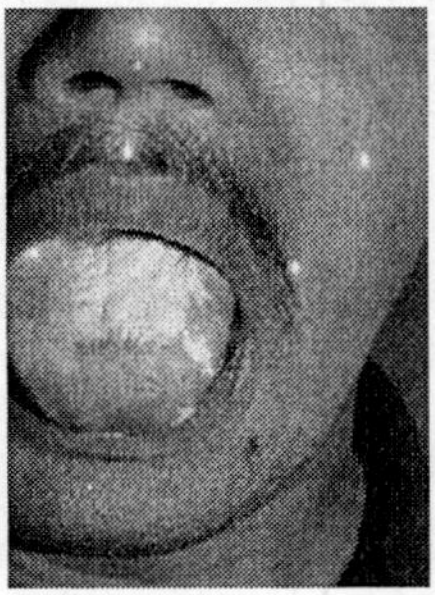

Thrush is anothe common infection usually develops in the gastro-intestinal track and skin of the individual persons. It is an disorder of

Candida, in which whitish curd-like deposit appear on the tongue in infants as well as adults with immune deficiency. Thrush infection of vagina (also called Valva Vaginitis) is common in adult women with itching and discharge accompanied by redness in genital area (or on the glans in male organs). The vaginal infection can be transmitted to the male partnera and vice versa. Vaginal thrush usually clears with pessaries such as Nystatin and Clotrimazole. Contraceptive pills, antibiotics can create conditions which encourage thrush. Avoild wearing nylon panties, tight jeans and a moist environments.

Vitiligo

Pigmentary disorder on ears

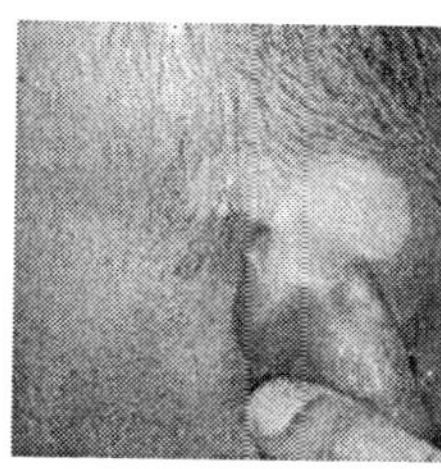

Pigmentary disorder on Breast

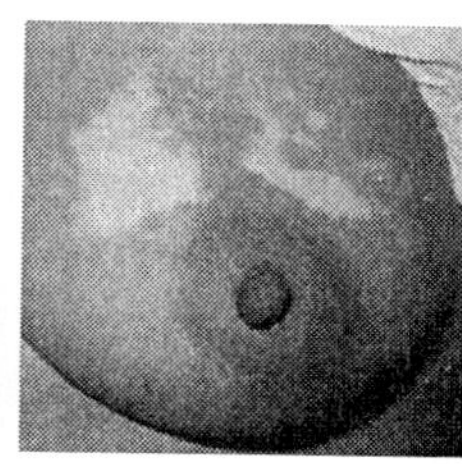

An pigmentary disorder of the skin when the melanocytes in the localised areas of the body stop producing melanin. The lesions vary in shape and size on the skin of body and spread quickly.

Diseases of the Hair

The scalp is nothing but the skin on the head which is similar to the skin of the body. Like skin on the body, the scalp consists of two basic layers - the dermis and the epidermis. However, larger and deeper hair follicles are present on the scalp. The hair is composed of a protein called keratin. The chemical composition of hair varies with the colour of the hair as carbon 50.56%, oxygen 20.85%, nitrogen 17.14%, hydrogen 6.38% and sulphur 5%. Full growth of the hair is divided into two parts : the root and the shaft. The rate of hair growth varies form person to person - the average monthly growth of the hair varies from 1/4 to 1/2 inch and the growth is maximum between the age of 20 and 30. The growth is faster in summer than in winter. The life of hair is cyclical - after a few years of growth, the hair become inactive and dies, then falls. The life span of a hair can be anything from several months to several years depending upon the health of the scalp.

Dry Hair

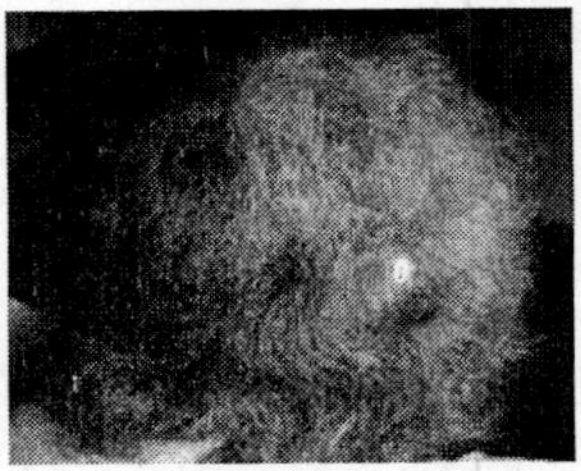

Oily Hair

Hair with Split ends

Overdry hair, over-greasy hair, brittle hair, premature hair loss, thin hair, split-end hair, dandruff, baldness and alopecia (patchy baldness), pelade, ringworm and eczema of hair are some of serious problems of hair which can be cured by Ayurvedic treatments. Dry hair looks dry, dull, lifeless and hair tends to loose its natural oil and moisture when shampooed. Dull hair has no sheen and may split at the ends generally due to lack of oil contents in the scalp. Give an egg mask to your hair. To do this mix two eggs in a cup of olive oil and rub into hair, then rinse off. Oily hair looks limp, too greasy and clumps together due to excessive oily scalp and increased hormonal activity during pubery and middle age. Wash your hair, then rinse with the tea and finally with cold water. Brittle hair, too, looks dry, lifeless and lacks manageability. In this condition, the hair may have many split ends and breaks when a strand is pulled between the fingers. Sometimes, white flakes appear on itchy scalp caused by hair dandruff, dry scalp and effect of weather. In case of thin hair (sparsely spaced hair), give your hair a warm treatments. Use warm almond, olive or coconut oil. Rub it with cotton wool, leave overnight, then shampoo the hair next morning. If the hair has many split ends, then massage into the scalp a solution mixing 2 tbs. Castor oil to 1 tsp. each vinegar and glycerine. Now steam the hair, then wash it off.

Hair Dandruff

Hair Dandruff—Tinea Capitis

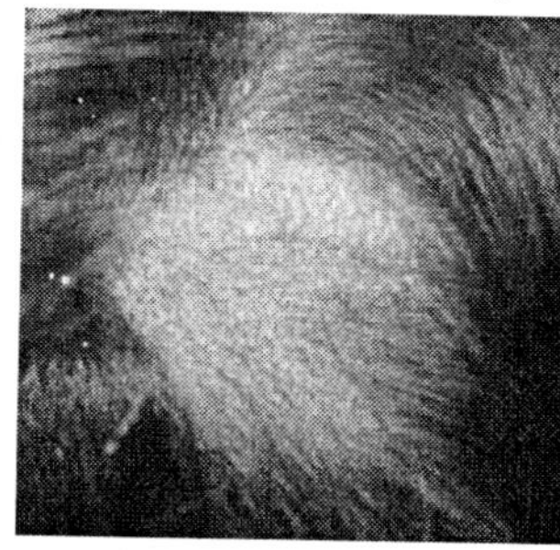

Dandruff is kind of Dermatitis — a thin scaly condition of the scalp caused by the hair follicle becoming blocked with excess sebum. Rough papules are seen with itching, without any discharge. Wash the hair every other day using a mild shampoo, then rinse the scalp in either warm water to which added 1 tbs. of cider vinegar or a strong infusion of one of the following herbs : burdock root, stinging nettles, raspberry leaves, sage, goosegrass, marjoram, parsley and rosemary added to soap wort shampoo. Another recipes to cure dandruff are : Mix 5 tbs of strong rosemary infusion with a pinch of borax and massage into the scalp daily. Massage the scalp with apple juice tonic three times a week. Mix together 1 tbs of pure apple juice and 3 tbs of warm water and massage into the scalp. Hot oil therapy is another method to cure dandruff. Massage hot oil into the scalp at night. Next morning, an hour before taking bath, rub lemon juice mixed with cosmetic vinegar into the scalp with cotton wool. Give the hair a good wash with egg shampoo. As a last rinse use lemon juice mixed to a cup of water. Continue this treatment for three months. A hot steam bath to the hair and scalp cures dandruff. Massage with hot oil and wrap a hot damp towel on the head like a turban so that steam may fight dandruff.

Premature Greying of Hair and Baldness

Premature Grey Hairs

Lack of care of hair, tendency to wash them frequently with hot water, malfunctioning of glands, chronic cold, after effects of high temperature fever (typhoid, scarlet fever, influenza etc.), lack of nourishment, effect of pregnancy and child birth, breast feeding, hormonal treatment, serious operation, severe trauma (burns and fractures), exposure of scalp to x-rays, hair perming, effect of chemical hair dye, pulling hair in a 'bun' or 'pony tail', taking slimming diets, prolonged mental tension, deficiency of nutrients in diet, anxiety, psychological stress, use of hair dryer and hot rollers and hereditary factors are some of the reasons of loss of hair and chronic hair falling. There are several Ayurvedic treatments to cure premature hair-loss. Some of old-fashioned preparations cure to halt falling hair which include steeping a sliced onion in rum for hours and using the resulting liquid as a massage. Application of hot oil conditioner is another remedy. Heat small quantity of olive oil or a herbal oil in a bowl and massage it well into the scalp until the hair is completely saturated. Cover your hair with a hot towel. Leave for overnight and shampoo in the morning. Dilute 3 drops of essential oil of cedar wood in 1 tsp. of base oil and massage into the scalp for hair loss and prevent alopecia. Three parts of eucalyptus oil mixed with one part of

Alopecia Aerata

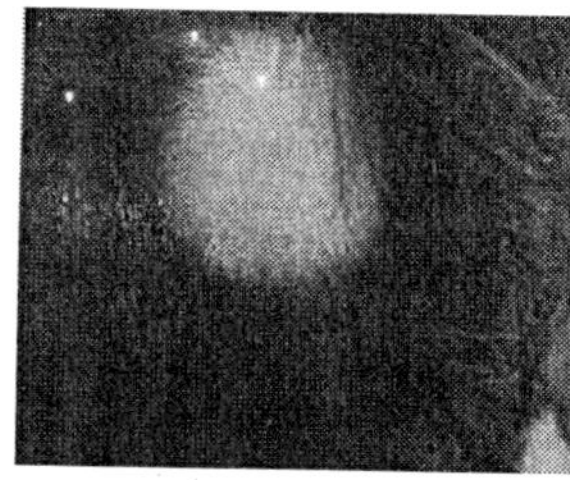

clove oil rubbed into the scalp at night. The **Alopecia** is sudden appearance of small bald circles on the scalp Eczema of the scalp also leads to baldness. Alopecia is generally of three types : Alopecia Senilis (usually occur in old age, in which hair loss is usually permanent), Alopecia Premature (slow thinning process of hair loss usually occur in middle age) and Alopecia Areota (sometimes occur in very young age).

Hair Dressing with roller

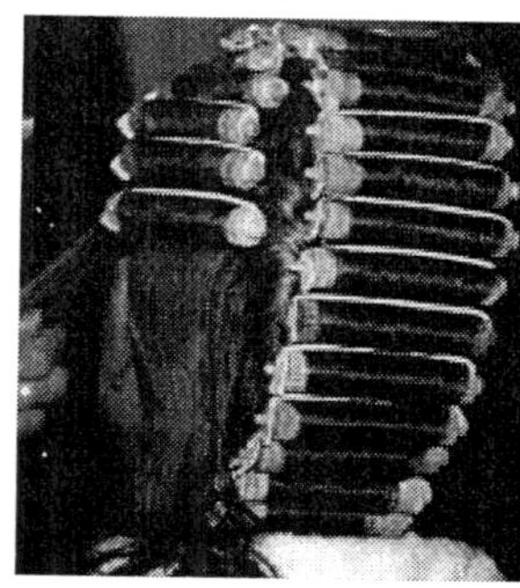

To cure alopecia apply carbonic snow (dry) on bald patches, which gives an alternate cold and hot feeling. Dissolve a few grams of potassium permanganate in few drops of water and apply on bald patches three to four times a day. Preserve mangoes in oil for about a year and massage the scalp with this oil. **Pelade** refers to several well-defined clear bald patches on the head usually in case of children in which amongst the apparently healthy hair some broken abnormal hair are observed during close examination. These patches gradually expand and the hair situated around the patch are often virtually dead and fall out at the slightest pull. Pelade is not a contagious disease, the scalp does not feel any pain nor any itching in the affected areas. The remedy to treat this disorder in a natural way is to leave a calming effect on the nervous system by the use of tranquillizers. To stimulate the blood circulation in bald patches by friction, massage the affected area with carbonic snow or tincture of cantharides.

6

HYDROTHERAPY

Ayurveda helps to readjust the human system from abnormal to normal condition and functioning by the constructive principles of nature. Nature Care stimulates the organs of elimination of accumulated toxic matter from the system and purification to better functioning. To cure any disease, the first and foremost need is to regulate the diet. To get rid of accumulated toxins and restore the equilibrium of the system exclude acid-forming foods including proteins, starches and fats. Change the diet to fresh fruits which will disinfect the stomach and alimentary canal. If the body is infected with morbid matter, a complete fast for a few days is necessary for the elimination of toxins. Eat less when you are sick; stick to a light diet preferably fresh fruits till the return of the usual healthy appetite. Loss of appetite is nature's warning to avoid burden on the digestive system. Have a fruit-only diet for a week.

Hydortherapy is an important factor in the cure of disease. To stimulate the vitality of the body use water in various ways at varying temperatures in the form of a pack or a bath. The application of cold water to the abdomen (An hip bath)- the seat of most diseases and disorders of sexual organs help to lower body heat and stimulate the nervous system. Hydrotherapy offers a simple natural method of abating several body disorders without harmful side- effect. The application of wet packs described below leave a relaxing effect. They revive dead skin and help maintain it in a normal condition. Exercise, especially yogic 'asanas' promote inner health and harmony and eliminate physical and mental tension, depression and fatigue. Ayurveda claims that in acute diseases, water treatment accomplishes all the beneficial effects without any harmful after-effects upon the body system.

The application of cold packs to the surface of body draws the blood from the congested interior to the skin, relaxes minute blood vessels, opens the skin pores, and facilitates the escape of heat from the body. In inflammatory febrile diseases the blood is congested in the inflamed parts, produces inflammation, such as Rubor (redness), Tumour (swelling), Calor (heat) and Dolor (pain). A cold water enema is helpful in inflammatory conditions of the colon such as dysentery, diarrhoea, ulcerative colitis, haemorrhoids and fever. A hot water enema is beneficial in relieving irritation due to inflammation of the rectum and painful haemorrhoids and fever. It also benefits women in leucorrhoea.

The temperature of water ranging between 40 to 60 degree F (4.5 to 15.5 degree C) is said to be cold, between 60 to 70 degree F (15.5 to 21 degree C) as cool, between 70 to 90 degree F (21 to 32 degree C) as tepid, ranging between 90 to 100 degree F (32 to 38 degree C) as warm and between 100 to 110 degree F (38 to 43 degree C) as hot. Above 110 degree F temperature, water loses its therapeutic value and is destructive.

Wet Packs

Wet packs may be applied to any part of the body. The different types of packs include Full Sheet Pack,

Spanish Mantle, Body Pack, Abdominal Pack, Chest Pack, Scotch Pack, Throat pack, T. Pack, Leg pack, Foot pack and Hip pack. Wet packs help to lower high temperature, raise a subnormal temperature, relieve inner congestion, promote elimination, relieve pain and stimulate sluggish circulation of the body. The purpose of wet pack is to lower high temperature. The wet pack must be changed to hot as soon it become dry but avoid an uncomfortably hot pack.

Cold and heating compress is an effective means of controlling inflammatory conditions of the liver, spleen, stomach, kidneys, intestines, lungs, brain, pelvic organs and so on. The cold compress soothes dermatitis and inflammations. A heating compress prevents the circulation of air and helps accumulation of body heat. After removing the compress, the skin should be rubbed with a wet cloth and dried with a towel.

Hip Bath

It is one of the most useful forms of hydrotherapy. As the name suggests, this mode of treatment involves only the hips and the abdominal region below the naval. A special type of tub is used for this purpose. The tub is filled with warm water in such a way that it covers the hips and reaches upto the naval when the patient sits in it. If a special tub is not available, a common tub may be used. Hip bath is given in cold, hot, neutral and alternate temperatures. In a cold hip bath the water temperature should vary between 10 to 18 degree C for the duration of bath upto 30 minutes. If the patient feels cold, a hot foot immersion should be given with the cold hip bath. Rub the abdomen briskly from the naval downward and across the body with a coarse wet cloth. The legs, feet and upper part of the body should remain completely dry during and after the bath. Undertake moderate exercises after the hip bath to warm the body, which improve digestive system and help to reduce extra flesh from the hips and abdomen. A cold hip bath is a routine treatment in most diseases which relieves constipation, indigestion, obesity, helps the eliminative organs to function properly, is helpful in uterine problems like irregular menstruation, chronic uterine infections, pelvic inflammation, piles, hepatic congestion, chronic congestion of the prostate glands, seminal weakness, impotency, sterility, ovarian displacement, dilation of stomach and colon, diarrhoea, dysentery, haemorrhage of the bladder and many other problems.

Hot Hip Bath

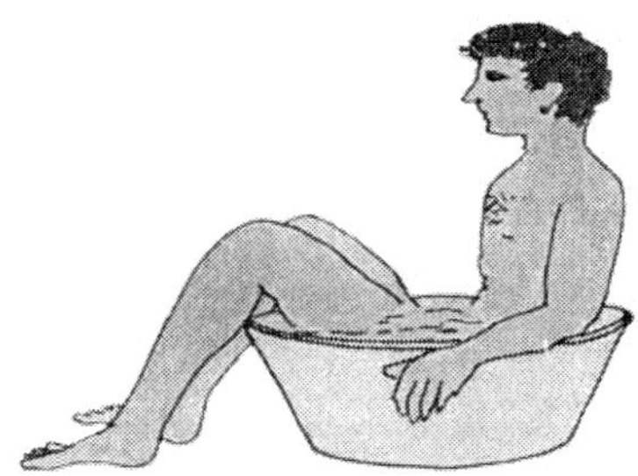

Hip Bath

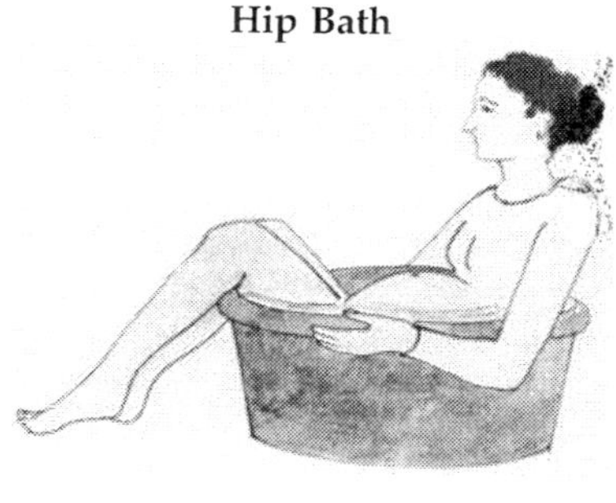

A Pregnant Woman having Hip Bath

It is generally taken for eight to ten minutes at water temperature of 40 to 45 degree C. Start bath at 40 degree C and gradually increase temperature to 45 degree C. No friction should be applied to the abdomen. Before entering the tub, drink a glass of cold water. Place a cold compress on the head while taking bath. A hot hip bath helps to relieve painful menstruation, pain in the pelvic organs, painful urination, inflamed rectum or bladder, piles, enlarged prostatic gland, painful contractions or spasm of the bladder. A cold shower bath should be taken immediately after the hot hip bath for better results.

Neutral Hip Bath

The temperature of water should range between 32 to 36 degree C. Avoid friction to the abdomen . The bath should be taken from 20 minutes to an hour. The neutral hip bath helps to relieve all acute and sub-acute inflammatory conditions.

Hot and Cold Hip Bath

It is also known as revulsive hip bath, the temperature in the hot tub should vary between 40 to 45 degree C and in the cold tub 10 to 18 degree C. The patient should alternatively sit in the hot tub for five minutes and then in the cold tub for three minutes. The duration of the bath should be from 10 to 20 minutes. The head and neck should be kept cold with a cold compress. The treatment should end with sprinkling cold water to the hips. The bath relieves chronic inflammatory conditions of the pelvic viscera such as salpingitis, ovaritis, cellulitis and various neuralgias of the genito-urinary organs.

Spinal Bath

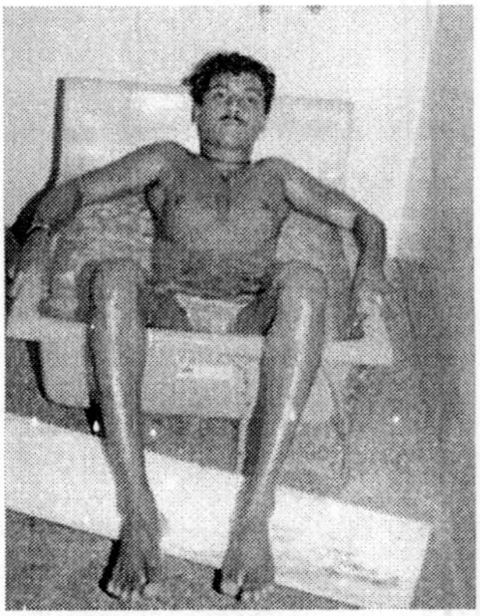

Spinal Bath

It is an important form of hydrotherapic treatment which provides a soothing effect to the spinal column and influences the central nervous system. Light exercises after the bath render excellent results. The bath is given in a specially designed tub with raised back to provide proper support to the head. The bath can be administered at cold, neutral and hot temperatures. The water level in the tub should be approximately two inches and the patient should lie in it for 5 to 10 minutes. The cold spinal bath relieves irritation, fatigue, hypertension and excitement It cures all nervous disorders, such as hysteria, fits, mental disorders, loss of memory and tension, vertebral pain and muscular backache. The neutral spinal bath is a soothing and sedative treatment and relieves irritation. The hot spinal bath helps to stimulate the nerves, especially when they are in a depressed state.

Foot Bath

involves standing in cold water for one to two minutes. In hot foot bath, keep legs in a tub or bucket filled with hot water at a temperature of 40 to 45 degree C. Before taking bath, have a glass of water. The head should be protected with a cold compress. The duration of the bath varies from 5 to 20 minutes. Take a cold shower immediately after the bath. The hot foot bath stimulates the muscles of the uterus, intestines, bladder and other pelvic and abdominal organs. It relieves sprains, ankle joint pains, headaches and restore menstruation among women. In case of cold foot bath, place three to four inches of cold water (temperature of 7.2 to 12.7 degree C) in a small tub or a bucket. The feet should be completely immersed in the water for one to five minutes applying friction to the feet during the bath by rubbing one feet against the other. A cold bath relieves cerebral congestion and uterine haemorrhage. It helps in the treatment of sprains, strains and inflamed bunions when taken for longer period. Avoid cold bath in cases of inflammatory conditions of the genito-urinary organs, liver and kidneys. Dry the feet with a coarse towel, followed by rubbing the feet vigorously with hands or walking briskly for few minutes. Another good mode of therapy is the bare foot walking in the dewy grass, followed by drying the foot and thereafter taking a brisk walk in dry shoes.

Steam Bath

Having Sauna Bath

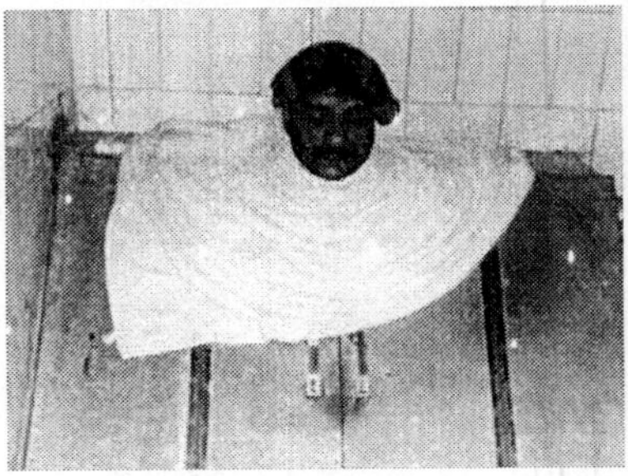

Also known as Sauna Bath - a western concept, is now gaining popularity in India and other eastern countries. It is one of the most important water treatments which induces perspiration. Many questions arise. Does Sauna Bath helps you to slim down? Is it good or bad for the skin? How long should one stay in the steam? What dress to wear when having Sauna Bath? In what position should you take this bath? Do not drink anything for at least one hour after having steam bath. Sauna alongwith yogic exercise and diet can do wonders in reducing weight. Sauna is a place to relax, to lie prone, speechless - in short, to exercise 15 minutes in Sauna is equivalent to running two kilometers. Toxins are eliminated through the skin in sauna bath, which helps skin problems like acne, dull, lifeless complexion and clearing cellulitis. Before taking bath, drink one or two glasses of cold water and protect the head with a cold towel. The duration of steam bath is generally 10 to 20 minutes or until profuse perspiration takes place. It is suggested to start with sessions of short duration, then gradually increase the duration when the body will withstand the heat for longer period. A cold shower taken immediately after the bath leaves miraculous effect. Have a 30 minutes rest at the end to attain the body's normal temperature. The dress worn at the time of Sauna session is generally briefs and bras or swim suit. A bare body will reap more benefit than a covered one. Do not wear watch and jewellery when taking steam bath, the steam and heat shall damage them. To sit up or to lie is another important question; it is preferred to lie on the back and wrap hair, so better wrap hair in a towel when having bath.

Epsom Salt Bath

Fill the bath tub with about 135 litres of hot water at 40 degree C. One to 1.5 kg. of Epsom salt should be dissolved in this water. Before taking bath, drink a glass of cold water, cover the head with a cold towel and lie down in the tub immersing the trunk, thighs and legs for 15 to 20 minutes. The best time to take this bath is just before retiring to bed. This bath is very useful for the skin beauty and disorders of kidney, sciatica, lumbago, rheumatism, diabetes, neuritis, cold and catarrh.

THERAPEUTIC HERBAL BATHS

Tap water Bath

It is good for skin, depending on skin type and the hardness or softness of the water. If your skin is extremely dry, washing face in hard water will not be helpful, the salts and calcium in the water will leave the skin dry. Use of a water softener such as bath salt or oil will help to counteract this effect. Be careful when applying cold water to breasts. Only douche the tips of the nipples quickly. Prolonged washing of the breasts could chill the mammary glands deeply causing bronchitis. Many women use ice to rub over the tips of the breasts. The intense cold causes a very strong static contraction in the mammary muscles without giving the time to cause a chill. Here are few herbal baths :

Milk bath is an excellent recipe for the skin, but these days it is not possible to afford milk for bathing. However, add a handful of powdered milk to the bath water. Rain water being soft is very beneficial, you may soften the bath water by adding a little sodium sesqui carbonate. Vinegar bath is very useful for itchy or dry skin. Add a cup of vinegar to the bath water. Oatmeal or Bran bath soothe and soften the skin. Put one tablespoon of oatmeal in bath water. Oatmeal and bran contain oils and vegetable hormones. To give the body skin feeling smooth and satiny, have honey bath adding a teaspoon of honey to your bath water. Starchy bath will leave your skin beautifully smooth, tight and soft. Mix a few tablespoons of laundry starch and a teaspoon of glycerine to bath water.

Lavender, hyssop, mint, borage, yarrow, rosemary and camomile are useful herbs for the skin used in bath water either separately or in a mixture. Mix two cups ordinary washing soda, two tbs. potassium carbonate and four to five drops of aromatic oil (lavender or pine oil). Use a tablespoon of this mixture in a bucket of bath water. Add almond or olive oil or sunflower oil to bath water. Baby oil or mineral oil should not be used as it cannot be absorbed by the skin. To prepare Bubble bath, beat one egg, ½ cup shampoo and one teaspoon gelatine and add the mixture to bath water when the tap is running. Milk and honey bath leave the skin feeling smooth, satiny and thoroughly pampered. Collect ingredients such as 2 eggs, ¼ cup each almond and sunflower oil, ½ cup olive oil, 1 teaspoon honey, 2 tsp. washing detergent, ¼ cup vodka, ½ cup milk and few drops perfume. Completely blend the eggs, honey and oils together. Add to the detergent, continue beating and add vodka and milk to make it thinner and luxurious. Finally, add perfume. Take the following precautions while having therapeutic bath. Avoid bath within three hours after a meal and one hour before it. Avoid hip bath and foot bath two hours after a meal. Women should not take any bath during menstruation. However, pregnants can take only hip bath till the completion of third month.

Sun Bath

Clears the skin of acne, heals mild infections, cleanses oily skins, gives a lovely tan and revives the whole body. On the other hand, hot sun bath can wither a dry skin, burn a delicate one, distend the veins, and cause burns and sun stroke. Sun bathing must be progressive, five minutes on the first day, ten minutes on the second and fifteen minutes on the third day. Never expose yourself continuously to the strong rays of the sun for more than half an hour at a time. To enjoy the beneficient effects of the sun is to play, walk or swim in sunlight.

Curative Power of Suncharged Water

Acute as well as chronic diseases such as Headache, blood pressure, anaemia, gout, paralysis, acidity, abnormal palpitation and convulsions, cough, asthama, T.B., ENT disorders, meningitis, liver disorders brain troubles, hyper acidity, gastritis, dysentery, constipation, piles, diabetes, irregular menses, leucorrhoea, cancer of uterus can be cured by white water treatment. Take about four glasses of white charged water (1ltr) at a time early morning before sun rise. Do not take water for two hours after breakfast and lunch. Start with two glasses of water and gradually increase the amount to four glasses. Different types of diseases such as cancer, constipation, diabetes, gastric trouble, hypertension and tuberculosis which can be cured with this method within two to four weeks (six months in case of cancer). Store water in copper container or an earthern pot. In case of cloudy weather it is difficult to charge water in the absence of sun, fresh collected tap water may be used within 15 to 20 minutes. Avoid drinking water in case of disease like dropsy, jaundice, ascites, rheumatism, rheumatic fever etc. Suncharged water or boiled water has no adverse effect on the health.

Turkish Bath

In this bath, the air is heated in a chamber having temperature 43°C to 54°C or a hot room having temperature 65.5°C to 76.5°C, followed by a plunge bath. The Turkish bath is similar to the hot air bath, but differs as the body is given friction to knead the muscles, and finally given a shampoo. Before the bath, the patient should drink 3 to 4 glasses of hot and cold water. The patient is frequently rubbed for one or two minutes to produce heat. To induce perspiration, apply a hot foot bath or a hot fomentation to the spine. When the patient begins to perspire, he should enter to the shampoo room. Rubbings and strokings are continued until the skin is smooth and polished. Turkish bath helps slimming and cures many chronic diseases. It is seen patients lose 800 gms or more in a single session of bath of an hour's duration. The Turkish bath should not be employed in case of a skin disease or diseases of the heart, kidneys and diabetes.

The Graduated Bath

It is a form of the full bath used for the treatment of fevers. The patient should be continuously rubbed to produce chilly sensations. The bath is administered every three hours. Persons suffering from heart disease should avoid a very cold bath. The physiological effect of the graduated bath is to reduce the body temperature and make skin healthy and glowing. Rub a cold towel after the bath.

Cold Friction

It involves the wet rubbing to the surface of the body with the help of cold water. The patient should be undressed, and made to lie upon bed wrapped in a sheet. The head, face, and neck should be wet with cold water and continued rubbing the body rapidly untill it reddens. Start with the front of the trunk, after that in succession the legs, the back, the hips, back of the legs, and lastly the feet. The soles of the feet should not be rubbed. Cold friction is employed in case of anaemia, chlorosis, tuberculosis, cardiac, dropsy, typhoid fever, diabetics, dicrotic pulse, subnormal temperature, pregnancy puerperal fever, chronic dysentery, malaria fever, coma, whooping cough, yellow fever, plague, dengue, influenza, lithemia, leprosy, emaciation, scurvy, rickets, purpura, anorexia, hypopepsia, intestinal catarrh, chronic nephritis, hysteria, neurasthenia, migraine, paralysis agitans and other drug habits. Cold friction should be employed two or three times a day.

The Hot Air Bath

It consist in exposure of the entire undressed body with the exception of the head to a superheated atmosphere having temperature from 48°C to 82°C. It may precede a cold douche, a cold wet pack, a cold immersion, a cold sponge, or a wet sheet rub, following the hot bath to increase the tonus of blood vessels and to energize the nerve centers of the skin. The hot air bath should be avoided in case of skin disorders, cardiac weakness, in the febrile conditions, in diabetes and in advanced cases of nephritis.

7

Ayurvedic Cure for the Genito-Urinary and Reproduction Organs

NEPHRITIS

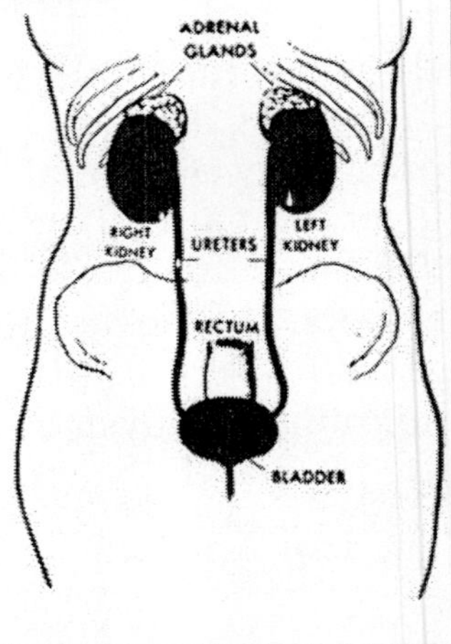

The diseases of the genito-urinary system include disorders of kidneys, ureter, bladder, urethra and the reproductive organs. In the urinary system, there are two bean-shaped kidneys situated in the lumber region. Their function is to regulate the body constituents - excretion of waste products and acid base balance of the body. The function of the kidneys is to filter the blood to remove toxins and impurities from the blood. The pure blood rotates back to the heart and impurities outside through the ureter in urine.

Renal Colic

Pain in the kidneys due to inflammation. To cure, two parts black cumin seeds, one part ajwain and a pinch of black salt are grounded together and mixed with a little vinegar taken in a little quantity every hour till relief obtained. Alternatively, as for applications, two egg yolks should be beaten in a copper vessel. Add to it Turmeric and a little water. It should be warmed and applied as poultice to the region of kidneys.

Dysurea

Scanty discharge, pain while urinating, pain in the penis (in men) and ovaries (in women), blood while urinating, heaviness in kidneys and urge for frequent urination. It is caused by cystitis, inflammation of the bladder and urethra, veneral diseases like gonorrhoea and enlargement of the prostate gland within the pelvis. Hyperacidity (excessive amount of acid present in urine) may also cause dysuria. To cure, desist from eating beans and pulses. Avoid eating green vegetable e.g. spinach, tomatoes and ladyfinger. Constipation should be avoided. Most important drug used for this condition is 'shilajita' followed by the compounded preparation 'chandraprabha vati'.

Stones

Severe pains in kidneys and bladder due to infection. To cure, drink every morning and evening juice of Radish mixed with Pearl Ash (jawakhar) for few days to break up the stones and expelled with urine.

Urinary Calculi

Pain due to formation of stone in kidney, ureter or urethra. Consult doctor for the treatment.

Scalding Urine

Burning sensation during urination due to hyperacidity or malfunctioning of kidneys. To cure, boil

250 gms milk with an equal quantity of water and drink. Alternatively, grind 50 gms of Rattanjot Booti (Onosma Echoides) with 5 grains of pepper in water. Strain and drink it after sweetening with sugar candy.

Polyuria

Excess of urine (amount increases in winter and decreases in summer) due to excessive intake of liquids or failure of sweat glands to function. To cure, eat any confection made from 100 gms of Black Sesame seeds. A confection from black sesame seeds can be prepared by mixing 4 parts seeds, 2 parts ajwain and 6 parts of jaggery taken twice daily in the morning and evening. Alternatively, the kernel of Tamarind seeds and leaves of horse radish should be ground together in water. Apply luke warm to the pelvic region.

Haematuria

Presence of blood in urine. Smoky or brownish colour urine due to stone in kidneys which scratches urethra. To cure, mix a pinch of Turmeric (haldi) in 100 gms dried Amla. Crush and steep overnight in water, which should be given to the patient in the morning.

Enlargement of Prostate Gland

The prostate gland lies at the neck of the bladder in men and surrounds the part of the urethra lying within the pelvis. The gland usually in late life increases in size in such a way as to obstruct the exit of urine from the bladder. The urine may come in drops and there is a feeling that it will have to go again. Modern medicine advises surgical interference. In Ayurveda treatment, the remedies mentioned under the heading dysurea above will help to some extent.

Diseases of Sexual Organs and Sexual InadeQuacies

Though many suffer from it, few seek redress while others ignore due to shyness. Syphilis, Gonorrhoea, Displacement of uterus, Leucorrhoe, Threatened Abortion, Phospaturia, Apprehension of miscarriage and Itching pain in vagina are some of common disorders in both men and women. These can be treated by natural ways. Sexual inadequacies is another problems sometimes in both sexes. In men, it mainly implies failure or incomplete erection of penis or premature ejaculation. In women, it is the lack of sexual response leading to an inability to achieve orgasm. Sexual inadequacy in men is usually called impotency and in women frigidity. Remember, frigidity is different from sterility which means an inability to produce a child. The prominent causes of impotency are some organic disorders, such as defective hormones, absence of or underdeveloped testes, an underdeveloped male organ (penis), severe diabetes, injured spinal cord, diseases of nerves and psychiatric illnesses (which is very common), excessive use of alcohol, tranquillizers, stimulants and some of the drugs used for the treatment of hypertension and mental depression. It is observed introverts, depressed, passive homosexuals and those who have an excessive emotional attachment to their mothers are most likely to suffer form impotency. A too submissive, too demanding or a nagging woman may also render the husband impotent. Several cases of impotency are occurred as a reaction to frigid women.

Syphilis (VD)

A contagious veneral disease to which the reproductive organs are susceptible which shows signs of decay resembling those symptoms caused by leprosy.

The disease is acquired by intercourse with a person suffering from disease. Ground in water 20 gm of Hirankhuri Booti (Corchorus Fascicularis) and five grains of pepper. Strain and take for two to three weeks. The disease has three stages: Primary, Secondary and Tertiary. Ulcer may appear on the whole body with vague pains in third stage.

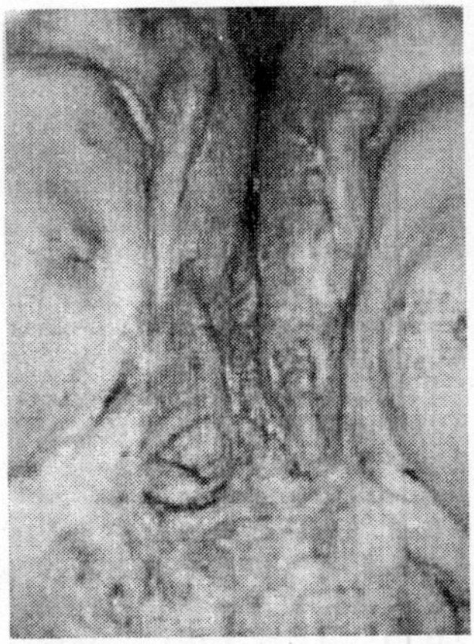

Infection due to Syphilis

Gonorrhoea (VD)

Inflammation affecting the mucuous membrane of the urethra in male and the vagina in the female appear. It spreads to other parts of body. Intense irritation of the urethra, pain on passing urine with which a yellow viscid discharge comes out. It is caused through sexual contact with partner suffering from this dreaded disease. To cure, seek doctor's advice. Hip bath in hot water is useful. The urethra should be flushed with a solution of potassium permanganate (1:3,000) with the help of syringe, which may be kept in the urethra for five minutes.

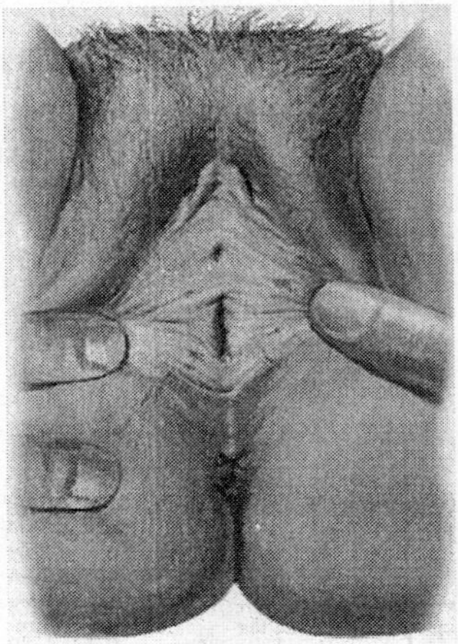

Infection due to Gonorrhoea

Displacement of Uterus

The symptoms are backache or headache with

heaviness in the bowels. Patient feels that something is sticking to uterus. The downwards displacement of uterus is known as prolapse and in this condition the uterus slips between rectum and bladder. The best way to deal with the problem is naturopathic way e.g. fasting, improvement in diet and exercises to tone up the muscles supporting the uterus.

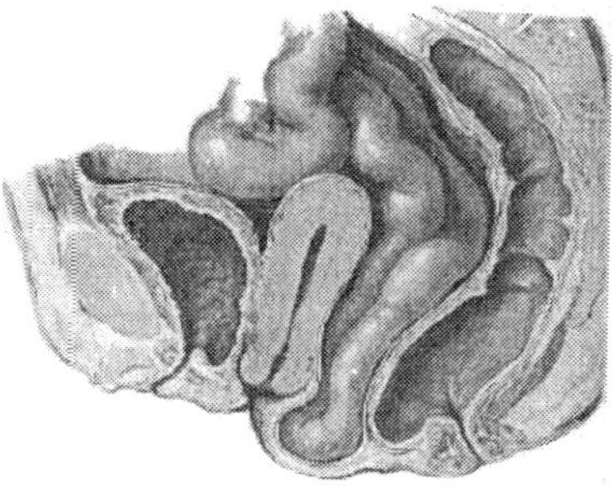

Displacement of Uterus

Leucorrhoea

The symptoms include white or pale watery discharge from the uterus. The discharge may be thick consisting pus causes infection or chronic inflammation of the womb, following child-bearing and a veneral disease. Exercise the body by running, playing and household work. Take every morning a dose of dried and powdered bark of the Mulsari (Minusops Elengi) tree mixed to an equal quantity of brown sugar with water. Avoid fried, spicy food and pickles. Late nights and sexual intercourse are taboo during the course of disease.

Nocturnal Emission

Seminal discharge during sleep usually due to

mental tension. Avoid sexy T.V. Programmes or watching adult movies.

Tumour or Sore in Uterus

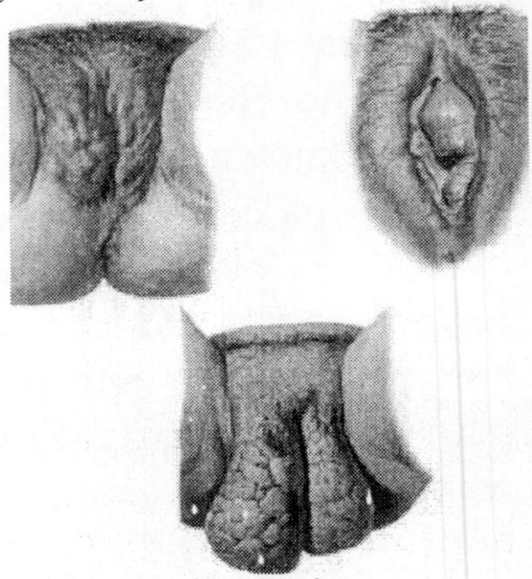

Vulvar Lesions

Lesions in uterus accompanied by pain due infection. A vaginal douche with water in which neem leaves are boiled. Fomentation of lower abdomen and the ovaries cure this order.

Threatened Abortion

Spotting (a drop or two of blood oozing out of uterus) due to heavy physical and mental work. To cure it take 'amla' wrapped in silver foil daily during pregnancy or a confection of petals of white rose.

Apprehension of Miscarriage in Pregnants

Threatened Abortion

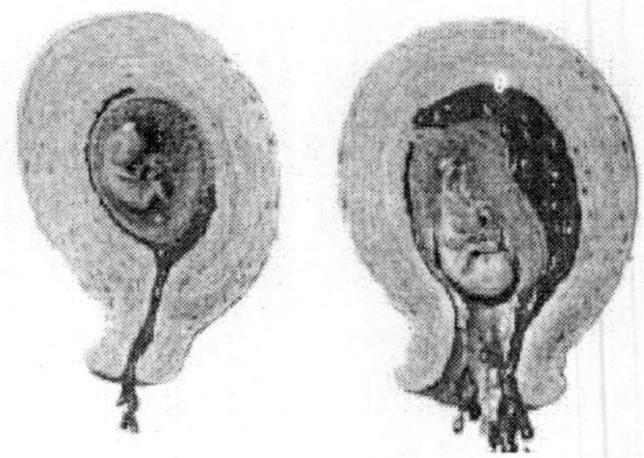

Pain or the slightest bleeding. This is due to excess burden or mental tension usually by the expectant mothers. The foot of the bed should be kept raised a couple of inches when the patient is on bed rest. A wet pack should be placed on the pubes for an hour in the morning and evening. The process should be repeated on the dates the pregnant woman would have had her period. After the third month the apprehension of a miscarriage will recede.

Faulty Functioning of Ovaries in Women

Amenorrhoea (stoppage of menstrual flow) comprises scanty discharge of menstrual blood or absence of menses may be due to anaemia, general ill-health, certain grave diseases like TB, aggravated dyspepsia, prolonged malaria and usually due to imperfect development of ovaries. Hot and cold hip baths and sunbathing will help. **Menorrhagia** (excessive discharge of blood or irregular bleeding from womb during monthly periods) has symptoms of giddiness, constant headaches and restlessness. The disorder may be due to the imbalance of the hormones and abnormal growths in the uterus. If the condition is neglected, it may lead to severe type of anaemia. Crush 50 gm bark of Ashoka tree and boil in 250 ml milk and equal quantity of water. Boil till half of the liquid is left. Strain, sweetened with sugar and drink. **Metrorrhagia** has excessive bleeding from the uterus from onset of the puberty or any age. A wonderful remedy for these menstrual conditions is Amla. Amla should be soaked in juice of green Amla for atleast 72 hours and then ground into powder, which is taken with cow's milk cures the condition.

Dysmenorrhoea

It is a sense of weakness and pain (in the groin) preceedes the menstrual flow - is a sign of irritation in the ovaries usually caused by inflammation of internal organs like womb, the ovaries or the fallopian tubes. **Delayed Menstruation** is the trouble generally seen in teenagers. Sometimes, the gap between the periods is as long as two months or more. Anaemia can lead to delayed periods. Sometimes, menses does not occur for many months at a stretch. Deal with the anaemia first. Eat leafy vegetables and fruit but avoid eating refined flour products, sugar and milled rice as far as possible. Hot and cold hip baths can help.

Ayurvedic pain killers during periods

Herbal teas such as dandelion, vervain, red raspberry leaf, fennel, camomile, caraway, angelica, yarrow, strawberry leaf, parsley, rose, safflower or linseed and peppermint are effective pain killers during periods. To prepare tea, about 1 tsp. herb is infused in 1 cup of boiling water for 10 minutes and taken three times a day. You may consult a naturopath for this. It can be taken hot or cold, with or without honey. To ease cramps, reduce stress. Here are two preparations for women during periods.

- **For Period pains:** Collect ingredients such as 15 gm each camomile flowers, mint, orange leaves, lime flowers and valerian root. Mix the ingredients together and add 500 ml of boiling water to it. Stand for five minutes, then strain. Drink three time (approx. 3 cups) in 24 hours (taken hot or cold, with or without honey).
- **Strengthening tonic during periods:** Collect ingredients such as 3 tbs. Juniper berries, 1 tsp. each camomile and confrey tea, 1 piece liquorice root and 700 ml water. Soak the juniper berries in cold water for 15 minutes and boil for 15 minutes. Now add to it dried berries and simmer until the liquid is reduced by one third. Discard the berries. Put the remaining ingredients into a warm China tea pot, then reheat the juniper liquid to boiling point and pour it into the pot. Cover and leave to stand for five minutes. Take half cup four times a day.

Premature Ejaculation

It is a malfunctioning due to psychological reasons. The male is generally found to be sexually more aroused than the female who needs a bit of foreplay to be ready for sexual acts. Too much of anticipation of the sex act, too much of excitement can lead to premature ejaculation giving a feeling of failure or lack of fulfilment which should follow the act of sexual intercourse. To cure this disorder, seeds of Lajwanti and sugar mixed in equal quantity, and the dose take every morning with milk avoid constipation and disorders of digestion. Proper exercise and a healthy living are also essential to cure.

Impotence (Sexual Weakness)

It is the inability to perform the sexual act which may be partial or complete, temporary or permanent. The problem can be categorised into organic and psychological. Organic impotence may be caused by lesions of the external genitalia, such as light foreskin of the organs and disturbances of endocrine glands (thyroid or pituitary glands). Ignorance, fear, weakness of sexual desire are the psychological factors which give rise to impotence among male. To cure impotence, tender seedless pods of Acacia should dried in the shade and powdered before being mixed with equal quantity of Brown sugar. Alternatively, tender leaves of Banyan tree may be substituted for Acacia pods.

Sterility (Frigidity)

A condition wherein a woman will be unable to conceive due to malfunctioning of fallopian tube,

Cervical Erosion

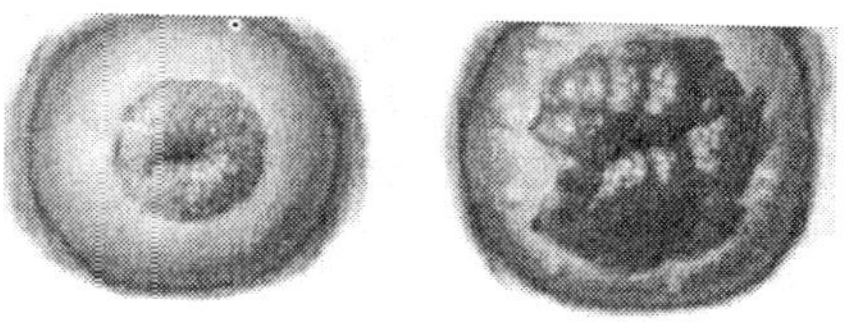

uterus, ovaries, hormonal imbalance, anaemia, blood poisoning and malnutrition. This disorder of sexual weakness may hamper the functioning to give sex pleasure or sexual enjoyment. As a cure, after the monthly periods, five ground ivory powdered should be taken with milk three to four days. Alternatively, roots of Banyan tree dried and ground should be taken in milk during night.

Itching Pain in Vagina

Intense Itching and Inflammation in Vagina

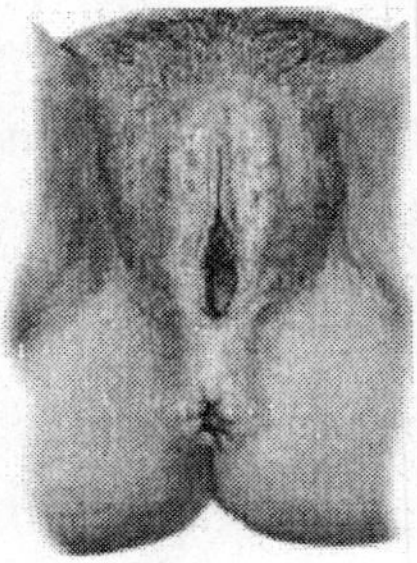

The trouble in women is common among those who have trouble of regular secretion. The itching usually causes due to semen remaining in the vagina after sexual relations. Too frequent sex should be avoided during pregnancy. Avoid too much scratching of genital organs and if the secretion touches the anus, itching, pain and swelling spreads. A warm water douche should be given and the genital tract painted with a solution of camphor in rose water. Avoid spices and condiments in your diet.

Flacidity of the Breasts

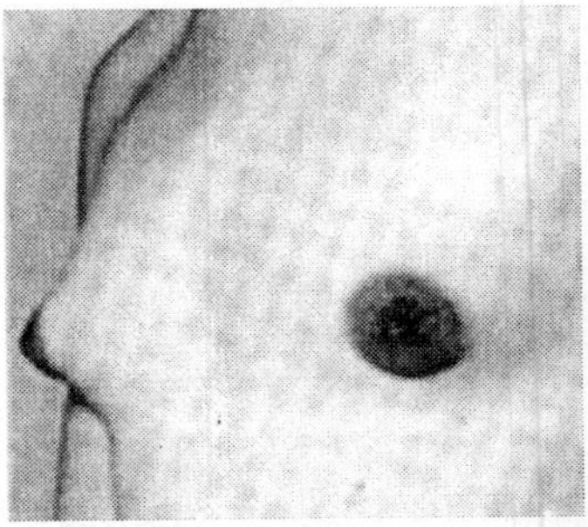

Under-developed Breast

It is caused due to changes in mammary glands or breasts of women, which develop when lactation has begun and are firm and attractive when a woman is suckling her infant. The firmness is reduced when lactation has stopped and when a woman has gone beyond the child bearing age. The breasts have a tendency to sag and become flaccid. To get relief, unripe fruit of Moolsari should be rubbed in water and painted over the breasts for eight to ten days. Alternatively, the tender aerial roots of the Banyan tree should be grounded with water, and may be applied as a paste on the breasts for a week or so.

Sagging Breast

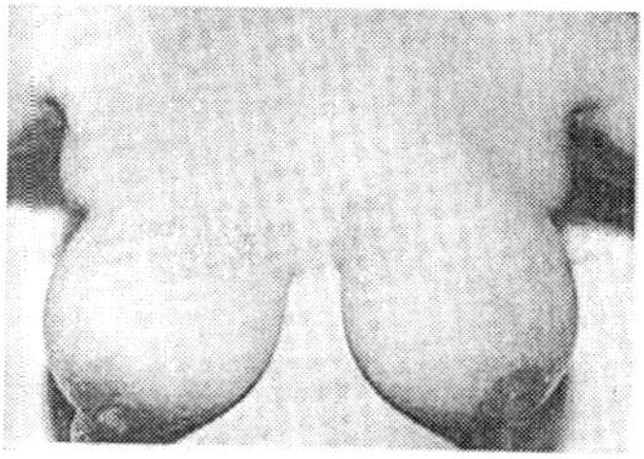

Drugs to be avoided during Pregnancy

Pregnancy is a normal physiological phenomenon in women, but it is accompanied by changes in the body giving rise to certain abnormal symptoms like nausea, vomiting and discomfort (morning sickness). In pregnancy, except for vitamins which are generally adequate in a good nutritious diet, no other drugs are ordinarily given. However, if symptoms of morning sickness become unbearable or there is unbearable chronic or acute disease, drugs may become necessary. The adequate use of drugs during pregnancy started in early sixtees. Since, most of the drugs taken by a pregnant woman reach the unborn baby in womb through the circulation of blood, which sometimes leave adverse effects on the unborn in the uterus. The nine months period of pregnancy can be divided into three trimesters of three months each. During first trimester, the cells of the fertilized ovum rapidly multiply to form an embryo which after a period of three months is called a foetus. During this period (especially upto 3 months), the effect of drugs may kill the embryo causing physical defects and malformation. During the second trimester of pregnancy, streptomycine may damage the developing growth of organs and bones. At this stage anticogulant drugs or large doses of aspirin may cause bleeding in the foetus. Drugs like barbiturates, morphine, pethidine or anaesthetics given during delivery may cause respiratory depression in the new-born.

Estrogens taken during pregnancy may cause vaginal cancer in the female. The new borns of addicted mothers may be premature and exhibit withdrawal symptoms. The chances of death among such babies are very high. Nitrofurantoin commonly used in urinary tract infection during the last few days of pregnancy may cause bursting of red blood cells. Oral contraceptives used by women for birth control, but if by any chance the pregnancy occurs, there is the possibility of adverse effects on the foetus. Phenytoinan - an epileptic drug taken during the last few days of pregnancy, the newborn may suffer from bleeding disorders (haemorrhage) and may cause physical defects in the foetus in early pregnancy period. Primaquine - an anti-malarial drug may cause jaundice and haemolysis in the new-born. Purgatives used in the treatment of constipation quinine in resistant cases of malaria and smallpox vaccination may cause abortion. Propranolol used in some heart disorders and high blood pressure may cause decrease of blood sugar in neonates. Large doses of vitamin A taken during pregnancy may cause developmental defects in the foetus, vitamin K if excessively used may produce jaundice and vitamin D may cause several disorders in new-born. Exposure to X-ray radiation must be avoided during pregnancy especially in the first six months may cause malformation of the foetus. Beneficial herbs used during pregnancy are Dandelion (Kukraundha), Fennel (Saunf), Camomile (Babina plant), Pennyroyal (Pudina booti), Caraway (Zeera), Yarrow (Sahas trapani), Strawberry (Raspberry) leaf , Fresh fig (anjeer) leaves, Parsley (Ajmod), Rose (Gulab), Safflower (Kusum) and Liquorice (Mulethi).

8

Ayurvedic Therapies for Emotional Disorders

DEPRESSION, RELAXATION & INSOMNIA

Cause nervous disorders in the human body. These factors contribute to the production of diseases such as headaches and migraines, neuralgia, paralysis, manifestations, suicidal tendencies, myocardial infaraction (heart disease), functional disease of brains, stammering, mental debility, coma, vertigo, hysteria, amnesia, nightmares, epilepsy, polio, cold feet etc. Many factors contribute to the production of nervous diseases. Some people are born with a nervous disposition, few are exposed to the fast pace of modern life which tends to bring on such disorders. Whereas certain organic poisons like the one produced in body by veneral diseases like syphilis and gonorrhoea sometimes give rise to serious nervous disorders. Chronic alcoholism may also bring on severe mental derangement. The depression is the most prevalent of all the emotional disorders which may vary from feelings of slight sadness to utter misery and brings together a variety of physical and psychological symptoms. Depression is the most unpleasant experience a person can endure. The growing complexities of modern life resulting crisis, mental stress and strain in day to day living usually lead to this. The striking symptoms of depression include sadness, loss of energy, constipation, loss of appetite giddiness, tiredness, sleep disturbance, insomnia, nightmares, itching, nausea, agitation, irritability, impotence and frigidity, aches and pains in the body, low body temperature, low blood pressure, rapid loss of weight, hot flushes and sensation of shivering. The main causes of mental depression are depleted functioning of the adrenal glands, irregular diet habits, indigestion causing compression over the heart and lungs, excessive and indiscriminate use of drugs and an excessive intake of fats.

The modern medical system treats depression with anti-depression drugs which however provide temporary relief but leave a harmful side -effects such as liver damage, hypersensitivity, insomnia, low blood pressure, headaches and dizziness, blurred vision, respiratory diseases and urine retention. Ayurvedic treatment of depression consists of regulating the diet, yogic exercise, scientific relaxation and meditation. Completely exclude tea, coffee, alcohol, chocolate and cola, sugar, food colourings, white rice and strong condiments from your diet. Morning and evening walk is nature's best tranquilliser which produces chemical and psychological changes that improve mental health, levels of hormones in blood and may elevate the brain chemicals.

Relaxation

It helps to control over nervous system and channelise mental emotional activities into restful harmonious vibrations which need sufficient rest and sleep. Learn the art of scientific relaxation and meditation which will go a long way in curing depression. Relaxation enables the muscles to work efficiently and eliminates fatigue by promoting blood circulation in the body. Meditation helps create an amount of balance in the nervous system, enable the glands to return to a correct state of hormonal balance and overcome depression. **A neutral immersion bath** (also known as "Full Bath") is helpful in the treatment of depression. This bath is administered in a tub fitted with hot and cold water connection in which the patient is given bath at a particular temperature. A **Cold Immersion Bath** is taken in a tub for 4 to 20 minutes at a temperature ranging from 10 to 24 degree C. A **hot immersion bath** is taken from 5 to 15 minutes at a temperature from 36°C to 40°C. The baths give relief to congestion of the lungs and activate the blood vessels of the skin muscles and treats obesity and chronic rheumatism. After the bath, apply oil.

Sleep

It is nature's greatest blessing of life which repairs the wear and tear of the body and mind. Nothing is so restorative to the nerves as sound and uninterrupted, and amount of sleep needed for an individual is determined by what he or she needs. Usually women sleep from 45 minutes to 60 minutes more than men. The amount of sleep required varies at different ages. For a new born 18 to 20 hours, growing children 10 to 12 hours, adults 7 to 9 hours, aged persons 5 to 7 hour. For proper sleep, however one should not sleep on one's back but on the side in a well ventilated place from noises. The bed should be neither too hard or too soft, but comfortable. The pillow should not be too hard or too high.

Insomnia

Insomnia or sleeplessness has alarming ill effect on health and beauty. Insomnia deprives the person of mental rest. Sleep gives relief from tension, rests the brain and body. The amount of sleep varies from individual to individual. Normally, seven to eight hours of sleep every night is essential. The most common cause of sleeplessness are mental tension, anxiety, worries, overwork, overexcitement, dull brain, suppressed feelings of resentment, anger, constipation, dyspepsia, over - eating , excessive intake of tea or coffee, smoking and going to bed hungry- all these irritate the nerves. Sleeping pills are not recommended for sleeplessness. The side effects of sleeping pills include indigestion, skin rashes and infection. To relieve Insomnia have a regular sleeping schedule (Going early to bed and early to rise is a good practice), fulfil the deficiencies of key nutrients (vitamins, calcium, magnesium, potassium and zinc), have a balanced diet and the eating pattern, divert the mind with soft music or light reading before going to bed, lie on your side, control breathing while you hold breath, carbon dioxide accumulates in the body and induces natural sleep, have regular exercise during the day and mild exercise at bedtimes (stimulates, eliminates lactic acid from the body and relieves stress and muscular tension) and application of hot spinal packs, hot fomentation to the spine, hot foot bath, immersion bath before retiring at night are beneficial to overcome insomnia.

Chromotherapy

The sun has the seven colours - violet, indigo, blue, green, yellow, orange and red. The violet, indigo and blue colours are creating cool effect on the body and are antiseptic. The three colours yellow, orange and red create heat. The remaining green colour is neutral. Chromotherapy has been very effective for treating various chronic and dreaded skin diseases. Violet colour cures skin lesions, tumour and baldness. Indigo colour cures ENT problems and facial paralysis. Blue colour relieves whooping cough, throat problems, cholera, typhoid, small -pox, mouth ulcer, problems of nerves, insomnia, mental depression and sexual weakness. Green colour relieves heart trouble, liver problems, high blood pressure and veneral diseases. Yellow colour relieves disorders of digestion, liver problems, diabetes and leprosy. Orange colour helps in curing asthma, bronchitis, swelling in trachea, gout, kidney, mental nervousness, epilepsy and skin afflictions. Red colour cures anaemia, sluggishness, paralysis, white spots, arthritis, T.B. and skin diseases. 90 minutes after the sunrise and 60 minutes before the sun set taking sun rays leave a curative effect.

The Rejunvenation Therapies

Siddha Vaidya, Shirodhara, Nasaya, Rasayanas, Siddha massage, Panchkarma and Sandalwood treatment trigger changes in mind and organs of the body to bring balance and harmony to the body. These adaptogens react in the body to achieve a state of balance. They affect the autonomic nervous system, the endocrine system, the blood pressure and help the body adapt to stress, achieve body balance, increase protein biosynthesis, elevate body enzymes synthesis, promote general endocrine synthesis, improve mental power, increase physical ability, fight free radicals, improve eyesight, beneficial to cardiovascular and respiratory system and improve specific resistance to various stressors like heat, cold , wind.

Shirodhara

Shirodhara is a process in which warmed oil is poured over the forehead and scalp. Shirodhara calms the mind, pacifies vatha, cleanses, calms and balances the nervous system, relieves stress and improves and rejuvenate the whole body. It is usually repeated three to four times a week for optimal benefit.

Nasaya is a procedure aimed at reducing waste products from the body. Nasaya is the introduction of medicated substances into the nose, stimulate secretion, remove impurities of the head and neck. It is used in headaches, sinusitis, nervousness, migraines, vascular headache, stiff neck, running eyes, ear infections, hearing loss and loss of smell.

Rasayanas is a beneficial treatment for the face and scalp to provide a head to toe beauty alongwith other treatments - massage (abhyanga), steam (svedana), pastes and masques (snehana), foot reflexology, aromatherapy, color therapy, Pancha Karm and Kriya Karma (rejuvenation).

Siddha Massage

Promotes relaxation, calming of Vitha, Kapha and Pittha. It balances and increases the circulation to body's largest eliminative organ - the skin. It increases lymph flow, strengthens the immune system and relieves muscle tension. Siddha massage helps to increase the production of collagen and elastin fibres, prevent wrinkling and increase suppleness of the skin.

Abyanga is recommended for muscle soreness, joint pain and stiffness, nervousness, tension, stress, lack of energy, restlessness, immune dysfunction, fatigue and tiredness, paralysis, poor digestion, poor elimination, sleeplessness and ungrounded feelings

Sandalwood Treatments is best suited for water retention, is diuretic and diaphoretic, leads to detoxification, releases toxins and acts as disinfectant, creates spiritual cleansing as well as cleansing the physical body, unlocks trapped fluids and toxins in the skin tissues.

Panch Karma-means '5 action' is an ancient scientific system for detoxification. It rejuvenate the whole system, bring youthfulness, strength the body and calms openness to the mind to clean the body, relieving waste materials in the body.

Shiatsu Therapy

Also known as acupressure, is used to treat disorders by pressing various pressure points on the skin of body. There are nearly 600 shiatsu points on the human body and a few are very important to cure disorders. Pressure on such points produces energy that flows in the body. It takes about 45 to 60 minutes to treat whole body. Keep both hands moving rhythmically along the meridians from one point to the other pressing on each point from three to seven seconds. Use the heels of hand, then repeat with thumbs to improve the circulation and induce relaxation. Press down either side of the spine, the buttocks and the back of legs with light pressure over the knees, arms, hands and legs. Press gently on all points on abdomen working clockwise in circles. Work from centre of the chest outwards, pressing in lines between the ribs. Rub hands, then stroke the oil on the body. Essential oil is very useful for skin, vigour and vitality.

Facial Massage

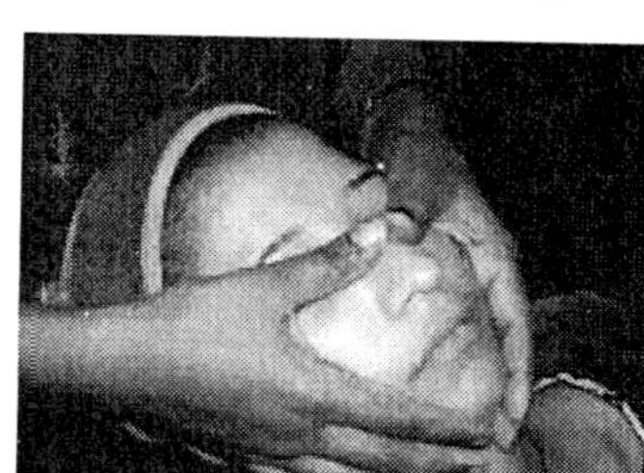

Massage Under the Eyes

Improves the circulation and energy flow in the face and tone the skin. Hold each point for five seconds. If you are suffering from headache and migraines, hold pressure points at the centre of hairline to the crown of head, centre between the eyebrows, on top edge of cheekbone just below the eye and below the end of eyebrows. If you are suffering from overweight hold pressuring points at the centre of groove between nose and upperlip. In case of tired eyes, eye bags and puffy eyes hold points at the inner corner of the eyes, middle of eyebrows and between eye sockets and cheekbones. Facial tension, nasal congestion and toothache can be relieved by holding small grooves at the side of the nose. If suffering from tired or sagging face, hold points at centre of lower cheekbone, outer corners of the eyes and hollows just below the ears. For energising the whole body massage at the centre of the palms of hands and in the middle of eyebrows.

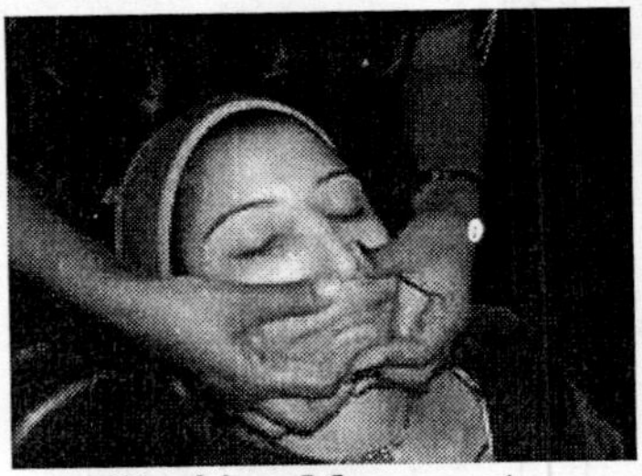

Stroking Movement

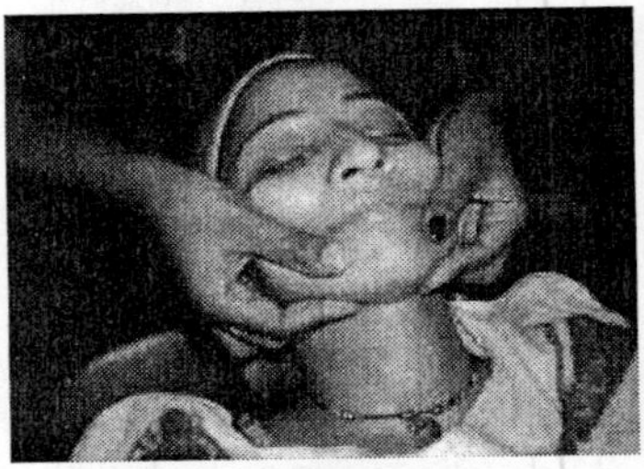

Pinching Movement

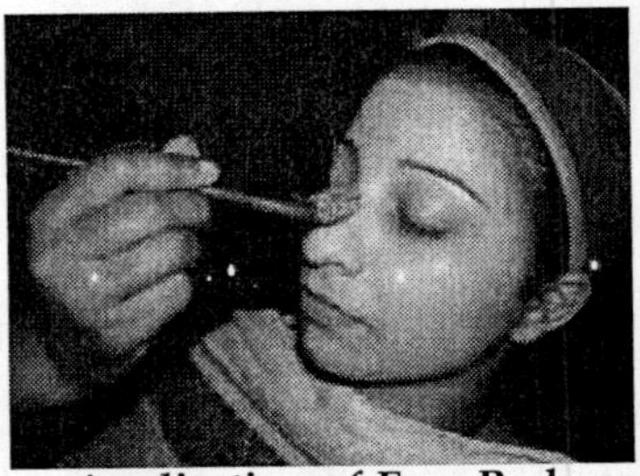

Application of Face Pack

Aroma Therapy

It is a powerful healing art that has profound effect on both body and mind. Aromatherapy makes use of the essential oils, which are extracted from the plants. Essential oil can be absorbed either through the sense of smell or if massaged into the body then through the pores of the skin. Essential oils are highly volatile, evaporating readily on exposure to air and when inhaled may enter the body. When dilute and applied externally, essential oil molecules enter the skin. All essential oils appear to be antiseptic and bactericidal to some extent and may also be helpful in treatment of viral infection. These essential oils have the potential to stimulate healthy cell renewal and growth and to regulate and restore balance to mind, body systems. Essential oils are the aromatic or volatile constituents found in plants which are light sensitive, heat sensitive, highly concentrated and have a characteristic fragrance. Essential oils are produced in different parts of plants e.g. roots, leaves, flowers, fruits, seeds, peel and bark. Aromatherapy increases blood supply to the tissues, which aid to beauty.

Essential oils have a therapeutic effect on the body as they are analgesic ; anti-fungal; anti-inflammatory, antioxidant; antiseptic; antispasmodic, antiviral, catmant; carminative; depurative; digestive; diuretic; expectorant, hepatic; laxative, hypertensive and hypotensive; sedative; stimulant, toning and many more. Essential oils restore balance to the emotions and mind, soothe nervous tension and settle a worried mind, calm anxiety and apprehension, improve concentration and memory, pacific anger and frustration, uplift depression and negativity, enhance love and relationship and strengthen the spirit to help indecision. Essential oils are absorbed by the body through massage or hydrotherapy. Aromatherapy provide the benefits such as induce deep relaxation, improve circulation to the muscles, reduce inflammation and pain, release neck and shoulders tension, cure backache, relieve neuralgic, arthritic and rheumatic conditions, promote correct posture, improve the function of internal organs, improve digestion, relieve constipation, increases the ability of the kidneys to function efficiently, flush the lymphatic system by elimination of harmful waste substances, reduce high blood pressure, help disperse headaches or migraines, stimulates mind and body without any side effects, help release suppressed feelings and stimulates the immune system.

Essential Oil Therapy

Essential oils penetrate deep into the layers of the skin due to their nourishing, cleansing and detoxifying qualities. These oils tighten the skin, increase blood circulation, calm the nervous system and support the skin's functions. For a Normal Skins camomile, geranium, jasmine, neroli, rose, ylang-ylang are beneficial. In case of a Troubled Skins (Irritated) cedarwood, eucalyptus, peppermint, rosemary are good. For Oily Skin bergamot, camphor, cedarwood, cypress, geranium, juniperberry, lavender, lemon, rosewood, sandalwood, vetiver will help, whereas for **dry skin** camomile, clary sage, geranium, lavender, jasmine, neroli, orange, patchouli, rose, rosewood, sandalwood, vetiver benefit. Rough / Broken Skin needs camomile, lavender, rose and sandalwood oils. For broken skin veins camomile, lavender, neroli, rose, rosewood oils. A sensitive skin requires chamomile, geranium, jasmine, neroli, rose and rosewood oils. For a inflamed skin camomile, clary sage, geranium, jasmine, neroli and sandalwood oils are extremely beneficial. Mature and aging skin need oils e.g. blue camomile, clary sage, cypress, frankincense, lavender, fennel, neroli, orange, rose, rosewood, sandalwood, vetiver and ylang- ylang. Birch, cypress, juniperberry, lemon, orange, rosemary cure cellulitis. **Stretch marks -** small tears in the skin surface, at first as red or purplish marks which eventually fade are caused by rapid weight-gain. Essential oils can minimize the scarring of the skin. Massage or oil body with essential oils once a day, specially at stomach, breast and thighs. Best oils for this condition are frankincense and tangerine, rose, camomile, neroli, sage and rosewood.

Essential oils - that heal skin include **Sweet Basil** which stimulates mental concentration, strengthens nervous system, revitalises the skin, useful antiseptic and cures respiratory infection when blended with herbs e.g. Bergamot, Clary sage and Geranium. **Bay** stimulates hair growth, relieves muscle spasm, improves circulation, relieves melancholy and nervous exhaustion when blended with Rosemary, Geranium, Lavender, Ylang Ylang and Citrus oils. **Bay Laurel** regulates the lymphatic system, stimulates the mind, heals bronchitis, relieves sinus infection and melancholy when blended with Lavender, Clary sage, Cypress and Frankinscense. **Bergamot** balances nervous system, relieves anxiety and stress, lifts melancholy, helps restful sleep, antiviral, cures cold sores, cures psoriasis & eczema and relieves post - natal stress when blended with Lavender, Neroli, Jasmine, Coriander, Juniper, Camomile and Lemon. **Black Pepper** has energizing effect, increases circulation, relieves muscle aches and stiffness, fights cold and infections, relieves rheumatism and relieves arthritic pain when blended with Rosemary, Lavender, Frankincense, Sandalwood, Marjoram. **Atlas Cedar** relaxes tense muscles, calms emotions, enhances meditation, eases pain and relieves hair loss when blended with Bergamot, Cypress, Rosemary, Juniper, Vetiver, Neroli and Clary sage. **Roman Chamomile** relieves muscular pain, used as a sedative, relieves nervous tension, helps with sleeplessness, used as an anti-inflammatory, relieves aches and pains and cures sunburn and rashes when blended with Bergamot,

Jasmine, Cypress, Neroli, Vetiver, Rosemary and Clary sage. **Citronella** relieves arthritis pain, cures digestive troubles and soothes and deodorise foot when blended with Geranium, Lemon, Orange and Bergamot.

Clary Sage relieves stress and tension, eases pain, provides restful sleep, relieves nervous exhaustion, relaxes body muscles, promotes oestrogen hormones and suitable for menopause when blended with Juniper, Lavender, Bergamot, Cypress, Jasmine, Geranium and Sandalwood. **Coriander** relieves muscular pain and helps nervous exhaustion when blended with Ginger, Bergamot, Jasmine, Neroli, Sandalwood, Cardamon, Sandalwood and Marjoram. **Cypress** increases circulation, relieves muscular cramps and painful periods, cures bronchitis and whooping cough, reduces nervous tension, used in footbath and relieves aching legs when blended with Cedarwood, Lavendar, Cardamon, Sandalwood, Bergamot, Orange, Clary sage. **Eucalyptus** relieves asthma. **Fennel** relieves neuro muscular spasms, cures arthritis and relieves bronchitis and cough, relieves stress and tension, cures ingestion & constipation, cellulitis and balances female reproductive system when blended with Lavender, Geranium, Rose and Sandalwood. **Frankincense** elevates mind and spirit, calms nerves of body, enhances meditation, relieves respiratory inspections, cures scars and boils, clears lines and wrinkles, anti-inflammatory, relieves mouth ulcers when blended with Sandalwood, Pine, Lavendar, Vetiver, Geranium, Neroli, Orange, Bergamot and Basil. **Geranium** reduces stress and tension, eases pain, balances hormones, relieves fatigue and exhaustion, tones liver and kidney and lifts melancholy when blended with Lavender, Patchouli,

Clave, Neroli, Sandalwood, Jasmine.

Ginger reduces muscular pain, increases circulation, relieves bronchitis, cures whooping cough, nervous exhaustion, heals cold and fever and stimulates appetite when blended with Sandalwood, Vetiver, Patchouli, Frankincense, Cedarwood, Coriander, Rose, Neroli and Orange. **Grape Fruit** relieves muscular aches, increases circulation, relieves bronchitis and stimulates appetite when blended with Lemon, Palmarosa, Rosemary, Cerdamon, Geranium, Lavender, Cypress, Neroli and Bergamot. **Jasmine** relieves muscular spasm, relieves painful periods, labour pain, anxiety, exhaustion and maintain healthy skin when blended with Rose, Sandalwood, Clary sage and Citrus oils. **Juniper** relieves exhaustion, cures inflammation, purifies and tones body, improves mental clarity, enhances memory, lessens fluid retention, disinfecting effect, cures cellulitis and cystitis (frequent urination), strengthens urinary tract and relieves infection and gout when blended with Vetiver, Sandalwood, Cedarwood, Cypress, Pine, Clary Sage, Lavender and Rosemary. **Lavender** relieves stress and tension, cures headache, promotes restful sleep, heels the skin, lowers high blood pressure, helps breathing and cures burns and sunburn when blended with Cedarwood, Clove, Clary sage, Pine, Gernium, Vetiver and Patecholi. **Lemon** balances nervous system, used as a disinfectant, purifies body, stops bleeding and reduces body temperature when blended with Lavender, Neroli, Fennel, Eucalyptus, Geranium, Camomile, Frankincense, Sandalwood, Rose and Ylang Ylang.

Mud Therapy

Earth was used extensively for remedial purposes in ancient times; it again has came into prominence as a

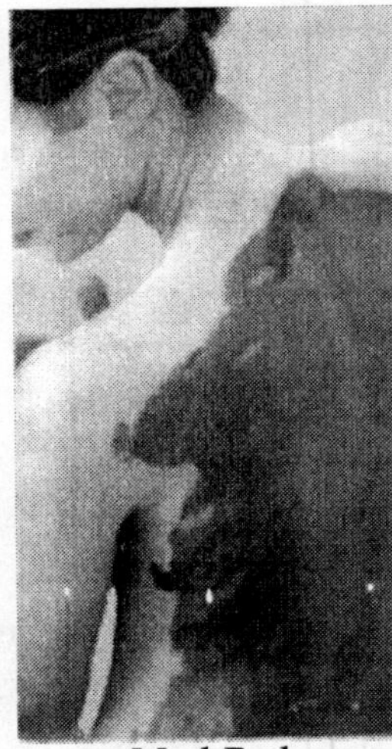

Mud Pack

valuable therapeutic agent. Earth have remarkable effects upon the human body, which are described as refreshing, invigorating and vitalising. For wounds and skin diseases, application of clay or moistened earth is natural bandage. It is advisable to go entirely barefooted on the grassy ground. The healing power of earth is very strong. This precious gift from the womb of earth not only refreshes, invigorates and revitalises the skin, but also helps in curing chronic inflammation caused by the internal disease, bruises, sprains, boils and sunburn. The cold moisture in the mud packs relaxes the skin pores, draws blood into the surface, relieves congestion and pain besides promoting heat radiation. A mud pack is prepared with clay obtained from about 4 to 6 feet below the surface of the earth as it does not contain impurities such as compost or pebbles. Mud packs have been found to be a valuable treatment for general weakness, nervous disorders, fever, swelling, eyes and ear troubles, gout, rheumatism, stomach disorders. Mud pack applied to this part of the body cures many disorders.

In another mode of treatment, the mud is first ground and then made into a smooth pasted mixed with hot water. The paste is then spread on a sheet which in turn is wrapped round the body. A mud pack is followed by a cleansing with warm water, followed by a short cold shower. The mud bath is found to tone up the skin by increasing the circulation and energising the skin tissues. Frequent mud bath improves the complexion, clears spots and patches on the skin and treats skin disease like psoriasis. The duration of the bath should be between 30 to 60 minutes as required.

Bare - foot walking on the earth

From 15 to 30 minutes stimulates the nerves of entire body. The technique is useful for treating high blood pressure, heart disease, depression and mental tension. **Sleeping on the earth** (Make sure to remove clothes before lying) helps for treating mental tension, abdomen/body pain, skin diseases, epilepsy, tiredness, hypertension, heart disease, cancer, anaemia and diabetes. **Sand - sun bath** also helps. Make a sand bed in open. Remove clothes and lie on the bed between 12 noon to 3 p.m. Drink a glass of lime water before sunbathing. Keep a wet towel on the head. The duration of bath should vary between 15-30 minutes. Do not drink water upto 45 minutes and food upto 90 minutes after bath. This is beneficial for curing skin diseases (leducoderma, eczema, varicose veins), myopathy, polyneuritis, inflammation of nerves, diabetes, rheumatism, sleeplessness, polio, paralysis, obesity and veneral diseases (syphilis and gonorrhoea). Rub mud/ sand (in ration of 60:40) on abdomen, breasts, legs, arms and other parts of body. Do not have meal for four hours prior to taking bath. Massage at night with coconut or 'arandi' or 'mahua' oil or desi ghee. This will help for body itch, side effect of allopathic medicines, high blood pressure, pregnancy disorders, anaemia, heart disease, depression, habit of drinking, body odour and skin disorders (leucoderma, pityriasis, urticaria and eczema).

Mud Bandage is applied on the head (cure headache, hypertension, high fever, sleeplessness and mental tension) and on the Spinal Cord & Genital area (has beneficial effect on the nerve system of brain, mental tension, anaemia, pregnancy disorders, obesity, impotency when bandage applied on male organs and frigidity among women. If applied On the eyes, It has beneficial effect on weak eyesight, watery eyes, glaucoma and puffy eyes. To prepare eye lotion, mix 25 gms pure honey with 50 ml pure rose water and few drops of lime juice. Put three drops of the eye lotion in each eye in the morning. It cures pus discharge, inflammation, pain if the mud pack is applied around ears. In case of severe condition, mix neem water or potassium permanganate or epsom salt in the mud and apply. On the breasts, rub with dry towel to stimulate the blood circulation in breast muscles. Apply mud bandage for not more than 15 minutes. It helps to cure respiratory disorders. When applied on abdomen and waistline, mud bandage is beneficial in curing kidney problems, dysentery, uterus disorders and menstruation problems. On the other hand when it is applied on female sex organs it is beneficial in the treatment of gynaecological disorders. The prominent disorders are connected with menstruation (scanty and painful discharge, profuse bleeding, irregular periods), vaginal discharge of white liquid laced with pus, diseases connected with pregnancy and childbirth, inflammation of prostate glands, spotting blood in the urine, itching at vaginal area and depression.

You must know that

Cotton seed oil is most commonly used for

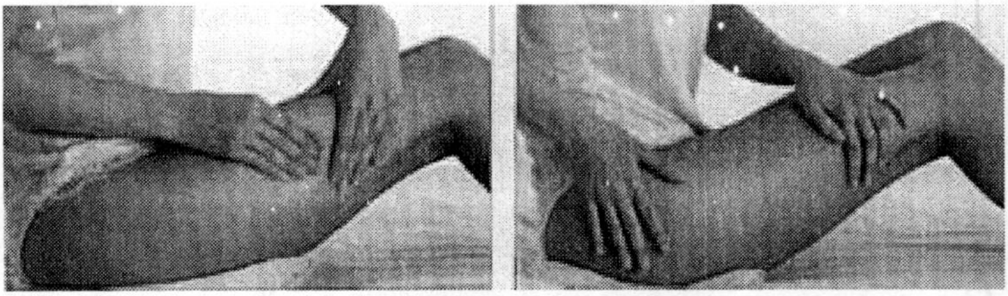

Upper Leg and thigh Massage

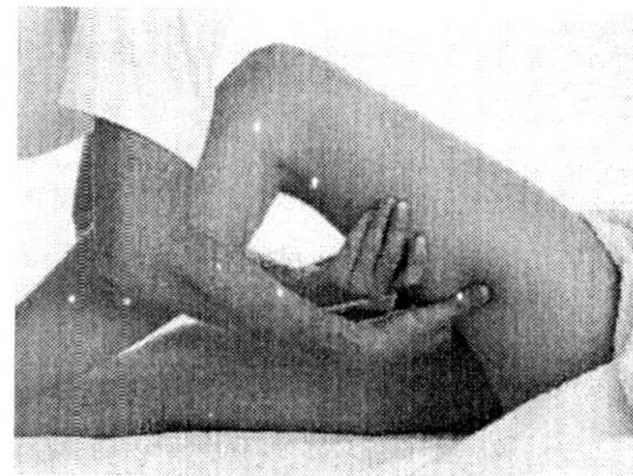

Thigh Massage

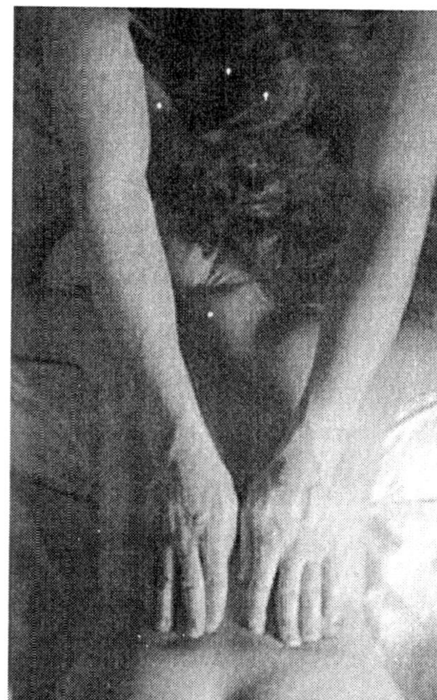

Back Massage

massaging. Butter is used for filling out cheeks, the neck and also for breast enlargement. Oil should not be used by persons with excessive body hair. The oil should be washed off completely after massage. Body massage may be done for 40-45 minutes. It is, however, not recommended in serious inflammatory cases of the joints and infectious diseases which cause formation of pus. Massage may spread the pus to the entire system. In these cases, affected part should first be bathed with hot water, then massage should be done for a few minutes. Avoid deep pressure on swollen nerves, for it will increase the inflammation. Sleeplessness can be cured by slow and gentle massage on the spine and back. Abdominal massage is beneficial in constipat-ion. It stimulates and tones up abdomen muscles. Abdominal massage should not be done in hernia, inflam-mation of the uterus, bladder, ovaries and fallopian tubes, kidney stones, ulcers of the stomach and intestines, and pregnancy. Avoid abdominal massage after heavy meal. The bladder should be emptied before the massage. Persons with hypertension should also avoid abdominal massage. Chest massage strengthens the chest muscles, increases circulation and tones up the nervous system of the chest, heart and lungs. Massage of the back stimulates the nerves and circulation for treating backache, rheumatic afflictions of the back muscles and for soothing the nervous system. Basic manipulations in Facial Massage are stroking (effleurage), kneading (petrissage), friction (deep rubbing), percussion (tapotement) and vibrating (shaking). Massage movements are basically of two types Relaxing and Toning. Relaxing movements are slow and soothing whereas Toning movements are rapid and energetic.

Massage Therapy

To obtain proper results from a scalp or facial massage, one must have a thorough knowledge of all the structures involved - the muscles, the nerves and the blood vessels. A skilful massage influence the structure and function of the body. On these pressure point massage activates circulation, secretion, nutrition and excretion of the skin. The frequency of massage depends upon the age and condition to be treated. Massage movements nourish the skin and its structures, reduce fat cells in the subcutaneous tissues, render skin soft and flexible, increase circulation of the blood, stimulate activity of the skin glands, strengthen muscle fibre, refresh (and soothe) nerves and relieve pain. All movements must be made in the direction of the lymphatic circulation - towards the heart. When massaging, the arms or the legs movement must go upwards from extremities towards trunk. For leg massage, keep the body relaxed, raised to help circulation of blood. Do not massage if you are suffering from any infectious disease, fever, heart ailment and after the seventh month of pregnancy. Consult a doctor, if you suffer from vascular lesions, varicose veins or haemophilia, dermatitis, mycosis, large ovarian, cysts, stone in kidney, hernia, recent bone fractures or dislocations.

Reflux Therapy

It has succeeded in several areas of disorder in which no medicine is required. The treatment is simple and done through the massage of the foot and helps reducing obesity and extra accumulation of fat on the body. There are about 75,000 nerve endings in one feet and the congestion in the body builds from the feet. The foot is a mirror image of the body which directly relate to the different organs. By massaging the relevant spots for few minutes every day has a miraculous effect on the face and clears muddy, dull looking skin and dark circles around the eyes.

Foot Massage (Reflexology)

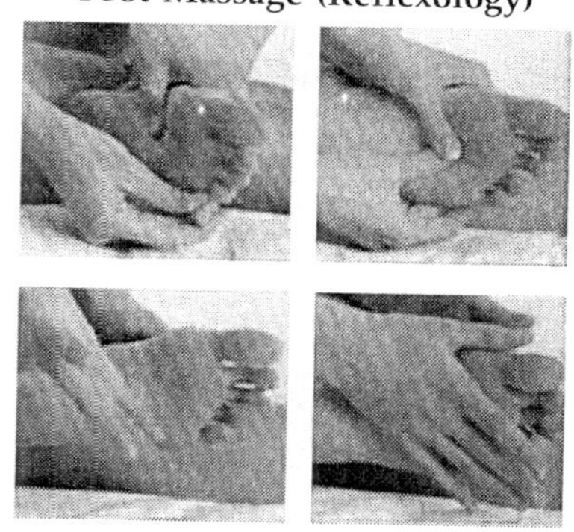

Enema Therapy

It is known as rectal irrigation. A enema involves the injection of fluid into the rectum. Lukewarm water with or without lime juice is used for cleaning the bowels. An hot water enema is beneficial in relieving irritation due to inflam-mation of the rectum and painful haemorrhoids. It also benefits women in leucorrhoea (white dis-charge). An enema with warm water 1.O to

1.5 litres should be taken daily when you are on a diet of fruits or are fasting or living on fruits alone. Enema can help when constipation is very severe. The following points should be kept in mind. To have enema lie down on a hard bed; the foot of the bed must be four inches higher than the head. You can take the enema while lying on the floor, but in that case

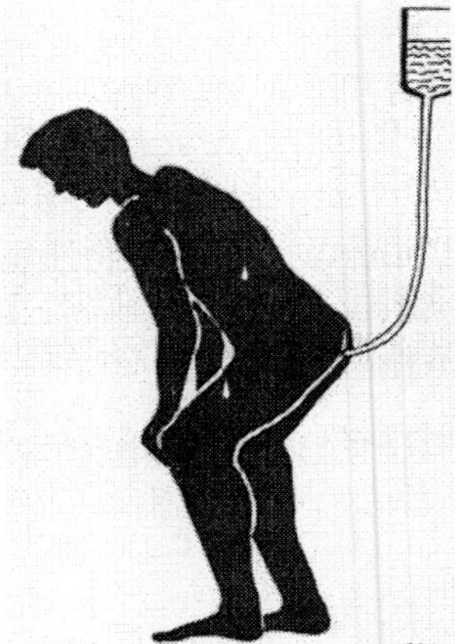

Taking Enema in standing

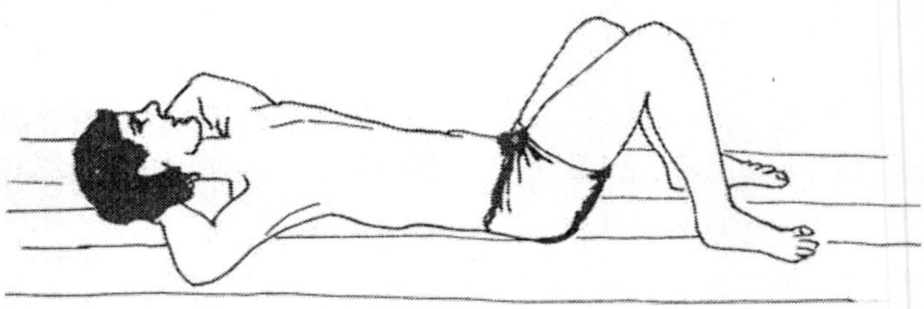

Lie after having Enema

buttocks should be higher than the rest of body. The vessel containing hot water for the enema should be suspended at a height of three feet from the body. The nozzle should be introduced in the rectum to allow the water to go in. Facilitate the introduction of the enema into the rectum. Let the water go into the rectum, retain it for two to three minutes before going to the toilet. Do not strain at the stools after an enema.

The Common Indian Names of Important Herbs

Aniseed	: Saunf
Asparagus	: Safed-musli
Almond	: Badam
Alfaalfa	: Lasunghas
Arsenic	: Sankhia
Arrow root	: Safed Haldi, Ararot
Apricot	: Khubani
Acacia	: Babool
Barley	: Jau
Birch	: Bhojpatra
Bay	: Kaiphal ka paudha
Borage	: Pathharchuri
Bilberry	: Bilbari
Blackberry	: Jamun
Black Babool	: Kikar
Black Pepper	: Kali-mirch
Burdock	: Beejkosh
Borax	: Suhaga
Beeswax	: Madhu-mon
Basil	: Tulsi
Blackcurrant	: Kali Rasbhari
Blackthorn	: Krishnakantak
Betony	: Chhitran Parni
Bergamot	: Zabir
Castor Oil	: Arandi ka tel
Camphor	: Kapoor

Coconut Oil	:	Nariyal ka tel
Cassia	:	amaltas
Celery	:	Ajmod
Caraway	:	Zeera
Clover	:	Tinpatiya Ghas
Camomile	:	Babuna ka paudha
Centaury	:	Bans Keora
Comfrey	:	Comfrey ka paudha
Cranberry	:	Karaunda
Coltsfoot	:	Desi Surakmukhi
Clove	:	Laung
Dendelion	:	Kukraundha
Dhatura	:	Dhatura metal
Eucalyptus	:	Safeda
Eyebright	:	Dadhi
Embilica	:	Anwala
Fennel	:	Saunf
Flax or Linseed	:	Alsi
Ginger	:	Adrak
Guava Tree	:	Amrood Vriksh
Hibiscus	:	Japakusum
Horsetail	:	Equisetum paudha
Hyssop	:	Zufah Yabis
Horehound	:	Pahariganda
Henna	:	Mehndi
Indian - Gooseberry	:	Anwala
India Aloe	:	Ghrit Kumari
Indian Catarrh	:	Chandarmol
Juniper berry	:	Hapusha
Jojoba	:	Jojoba

Jasmine	:	Chameli
Kaner	:	Leander
Lettuce	:	Chukandar
Leek	:	Lasoon Vilayati
Lavender	:	Plant Flower
Long Pepper	:	Pipli
Lungwort	:	Laungkai
Liquorice	:	Mulethi
Life Plant	:	Patharchur
Marigold	:	Gainda ka Phool
Marsh Mallow	:	Kanghi
Mind	:	Pudina
Musli	:	Dholi musli
Myrrh	:	Lohban
Morgosa Tree	:	Neem
Myrtel	:	Mehandi Plant, Bach
Marjoram	:	Marwa, Sathra
Neroli	:	Narangi ke Phulon ka tel
Nettle	:	Bichhubooti
Nut grass	:	Nagarmotha
Orris	:	Kewra
Oak	:	Majuphal
Oat	:	Jai
Plantage	:	Isabgol
Parsley	:	Ajmod, Prajmoda
Parsnip	:	Chukandar
Pennyroyal	:	Pudina botti
Plantain	:	Kela
Pomegrate	:	Anar
Prunes	:	Sukha Alucha
Rawanberry	:	Bobia

Rue	:	Brahmi Booti
Saraca Asoca	:	Ashok
Sesama	:	Til
Sage	:	Sefakus, saliva
St. John's Wort	:	Basant
Safflower	:	Kusum
Soapwort	:	Saboonbooti
Sloe	:	Jungli Alucha
Sheesham	:	Red Wood
Satyansi	:	Pela Dhatura
Shahtara	:	Pitpapda
Saffron	:	Keshar
Soapwort Extract	:	Saboonbooti
Sandalwood	:	Chandan
Shoe Flower	:	Gurhal
Sarsaparilla	:	Anantmul, Saalsa
Tamarind	:	Imli
Thymol	:	Ajwain
Thyme	:	Ban Ajwain
Valerian	:	Mushakbala, Jalakan
Vinca Rosea	:	Chandni
Violet	:	Benafsha
Walnut	:	Akhrot
Watercress	:	Jal Khumbi
Wintergreen	:	Gandhpura
Witch Hazel	:	Hamemalis
Worm Wood	:	Nagdon, Nagadamani
Winter Cherry	:	Asgandh
Yarrow	:	Gandana, Sahastrapani
Ylang Ylang	:	Karumugai